the on-t
on-target
manager

Other titles in this series:

THE ONE MINUTE MANAGER
Ken Blanchard and Spencer Johnson

PUTTING THE ONE MINUTE MANAGER TO WORK
Ken Blanchard and Robert Lorber

THE ONE MINUTE SALES PERSON
Spencer Johnson

LEADERSHIP AND THE ONE MINUTE MANAGER
Ken Blanchard, Patricia Zigarmi and Drea Zigarmi

THE ONE MINUTE MANAGER MEETS THE MONKEY
Ken Blanchard, William Oncken Jr. and Hal Burrows

THE ONE MINUTE MANAGER BUILDS HIGH PERFORMING TEAMS
Ken Blanchard, Donald Carew and Eunice Parisi-Carew

RAVING FANS!
Ken Blanchard and Sheldon Bowles

GUNG HO!
Ken Blanchard and Sheldon Bowles

BIG BUCKS!
Ken Blanchard and Sheldon Bowles

HIGH FIVE!
Ken Blanchard, Sheldon Bowles, Don Carew and Eunice Parisi-Carew

LEADERSHIP BY THE BOOK
Ken Blanchard, Bill Hybels and Phil Hodges

THE LITTLE BOOK OF COACHING
Ken Blanchard and Don Shula

THE ONE MINUTE APOLOGY
Ken Blanchard and Margret McBride

THE ONE MINUTE FATHER
Spencer Johnson

THE ONE MINUTE MOTHER
Spencer Johnson

THE ONE MINUTE GOLFER
Ken Blanchard

THE ONE MINUTE MANAGER BALANCES WORK AND LIFE
Ken Blanchard, D.W. Edington and Marjorie Blanchard

the on-time, on-target manager

how a 'last-minute manager' conquered procrastination

KEN BLANCHARD
STEVE GOTTRY

HarperCollins*Publishers*

This edition produced for The Book People Ltd.,
Hall Wood Avenue, Haydock, St Helens, WA11 9UL

Grateful acknowledgement is made to reprint the following: "Turn! Turn Turn!" ("To Everything There Is a Season"), words from the *Book of Ecclesiastes*, adaptation and music by Pete Seeger. TRO—© Copyright 1962 (Renewed), Melody Trails, Inc., New York, NY. Used by permission.

HarperCollins*Publishers*
77–85 Fulham Palace Road
Hammersmith, London W6 8JB

www.harpercollins.co.uk

This paperback edition published 2005
1

First published by HarperCollins*Publishers* 2004

ISBN 9780007811298

Designed by Nancy Singer Olaguera

Printed and bound in Great Britain by
Clays Ltd, St Ives plc

To all who want to take charge of
their lives and become everything
they want to be

Contents

Foreword

Just as sports teams have winning seasons and losing seasons, so do organizations of every kind.

And just as any sports team can experience setbacks and injuries, so can any business. Often, the most devastating cause of these is procrastination. A member of your team who is habitually late can cause tremendous harm to other players. It could be in the form of added stress for everyone, financial loss, or even failure of the enterprise. Thankfully, there is a solution to this problem—and you are holding it in your hands!

Ken Blanchard and Steve Gottry have knocked it out of the park with *The On-Time, On-Target Manager.* This book not only offers a rock solid plan to help procrastinators get on track, but it also provides a foundation for making day-to-day decisions based on the highest moral and ethical standards.

It's only natural for sports fans to hope that their favorite team will have a winning season each year. Similarly, shareholders, employees, and customers expect that their company or nonprofit is going to prosper and grow year after year.

Yet both of these expectations are unrealistic—even if top-quality leadership is in place. Having a great manager of, say, a baseball club does not necessarily guarantee a winning record or a play-off berth. Too many other factors come into play. The short list would include the strength of the competition, the nature of the schedule, and injuries to players.

Strong competition is a major factor in any sport. A baseball team that has hitters such as Babe Ruth, Lou Gehrig, Willie Mays, Henry (Hank) Aaron, Stan Musial, Reggie Jackson, Mark McGuire, Sammy Sosa, or Barry Bonds is likely to enjoy success. A team that has pitching strength—with the likes of Cy Young, Nolan Ryan, Don Sutton, Bert Blyleven, Roger Clemens, Randy Johnson, or Curt Schilling—is going to win games. They have a competitive edge. That makes it tough for the home team. Add a tough schedule in a tough division, and things become even more challenging. Mix in injuries to key players, and many of the fans are going to be unhappy with the way the season will likely play out.

I'm sure you can easily see the parallels in the world of business, education, and nonprofit organizations.

Competition will always be keen. Your "pitchers"—salespeople—are going to be pitching against some of the best in the business. Some heavy hitter out there is going to do everything possible to out-design your products, undercut your prices, or perform better in terms of service. By putting Blanchard and Gottry's on-time, on-target principles into practice, you and your team will be in a strong position to go for the win. No matter who you are or what you do, you will gain powerful insights from this quick-read book.

—*Jerry Colangelo,* chairman and CEO,
Arizona Diamondbacks and Phoenix Suns

Introduction

This book may not apply to you at all. But chances are, it applies to someone you know. A coworker. A direct report. Your boss. Possibly even your spouse or one of your kids.

This book is about a diabolical career killer that is lurking out there every day. In fact, it's far worse than a career killer. It destroys organizations, marriages, families, relationships, fortunes . . . even entire lives.

It's called "procrastination." In just five letters, it's known as "delay." It's when you put off doing something until later. But, as we said, this may not apply to you.

The rest of us, though, have battled with this insidious enemy at one time or another. When we were in high school or college, we waited until the last minute to write an important paper or study for a final exam. Then we stayed up all night to do our duty—and we barely functioned the next day.

On the job, we sometimes even miss important deadlines as the result of procrastination. Or we accomplish all of the meaningless tasks before we get to the important things.

In our homes, we're often too busy or too tired to read stories to our children. "It won't hurt anything if I wait until a better time," we tell ourselves. Then, when they're in college, we wonder why the "better time" never materialized.

We rationalize, justify, and explain. As a result, our jobs, spouses, children, and health all suffer. All because we "put it off" or do the "leastest" first and the most important last—if at all.

Although this may not apply to you, you should be aware that procrastination is far more universal than you might imagine. It isn't a condition that pops up out of the blue, either. It has roots that run deep and must be understood.

People often procrastinate because they don't have a clear picture of what's important. And knowing what's important involves knowing where they've been, where they are now, and where they are headed.

They procrastinate because they don't understand that delaying action can lead to poor decisions and poor performance—and separate them from good results.

They procrastinate because, while they are interested in getting certain things done, they lack a commitment to broader goals, higher ideals, more important tasks, and other people. There is an enormous difference between being interested in something and being committed to it. Consider the matter of exercise. Interested people will make all sorts of excuses as to why "today" isn't the right day to work out. "I'm tired, it's raining, I have too much going on in my life right now, missing one day (or week or month) won't hurt." In contrast, the committed people don't know about excuses: they only know about results. "This is something I'm going to do for myself. If it's too hot or it's raining, I'll do a speed-walk in a shopping mall."

It all comes down to three concise issues:

- Lateness,
- poor-quality work, and
- the stress that results from procrastination.

That's the problem in a nutshell.

The solution is found in the pages of this book—in the story of "Bob the Manager," who discovered the Three P Strategy and gained victory over procrastination to become on-time and on-target in every area of his life.

The first "P" helped Bob conquer lateness.

The second "P" gave him the keys to improved quality.

The third "P" helped him reduce stress for himself and his coworkers.

Right now, you might be thinking of a person—or several people—who could benefit from our message. But the question is, how do you give this book to people without offending them?

Our answer is very straightforward. You explain that while they may not be procrastinators, *The On-Time, On-Target Manager* offers a strategy that will make them more effective in every area of pursuit. Tell them, "The Three P Strategy even worked for the two guys who wrote the book." Yes, we are both natural born procrastinators, we have applied these simple techniques in our own daily lives, and they have made a difference.

This statement is obviously true. After all, we actually finished writing the book and even delivered the manuscript to our publisher on time!

Do yourself (if you're a procrastinator) and the special people in your life a favor—share the powerful message of *The On-Time, On-Target Manager.*

—Ken Blanchard and Steve Gottry

ONE

Late for a Very Important Date

Bob the Manager woke up earlier than usual one Monday morning. He always set his alarm for 6:00 A.M. so he had time for a half-hour walk around the small lake that was two short blocks from his house. This day, though, his alarm went off at 5:30 A.M. That's because he had a 7:30 A.M. breakfast meeting with his boss, Dave.

Bob was a little apprehensive about the meeting. He wasn't sure his longtime dream of being promoted from Team Manager to Group Manager was coming true, or if the meeting would spiral downward into an unwelcome discussion of a few minor "performance issues" in his past.

In any event, by rolling out of bed a half hour earlier, he'd have time for his walk and would still be able to make the meeting on time.

Bob completed his brisk walk, took a quick shower, sprayed on his favorite cologne, got dressed, and tied a perfect knot in his most "corporate" tie. He hadn't worn a tie for several years—what with the advent of relaxed dress codes in the business world—so he struggled a bit with that stupid knot.

Then he strapped on his very expensive, highly accurate Swiss watch and noted the time. *Oops!* He was running a tad behind. Getting dressed "just right" had taken more time than he'd anticipated.

Not to worry, Bob the Manager thought. *I can make up some time on the road,* he assured himself. He threw his PDA—his palmtop computer—and his sleek aluminum-clad laptop into his computer bag and got into his car.

He glanced at his watch again. He compared it with the clock in the car. *Yep. Still running behind. Better call Dave.*

When he reached the next red light, Bob the Manager dug through his computer bag, found his PDA, looked up the number, and called his boss.

"Dave here," said the voice on the other end.

"Dave, this is Bob. I'm running a little behind. Are you at the restaurant yet?"

"Yes," said the voice. "And so far, you're fifteen minutes late."

"I know. I've run into traffic," Bob said, even though he knew that traffic this day was no worse than usual. He could easily have allowed for it if he had thought things through ahead of time. "I'll get there as soon as possible."

"Good," said Dave. "I've got a full day going here."

When Bob arrived, he parked his car and practically ran to the door. He was out of breath when he walked inside and scanned the restaurant for Dave.

"About time," Dave said when Bob approached the table.

"Sorry, Dave. I hate to keep you waiting," Bob huffed and puffed, still gasping for oxygen. He took his seat and looked at Dave with considerable embarrassment.

Dave hesitated for an uncomfortable length of time before he finally responded. "Bob, how long have you been with Algalon Micro?"

"Six . . . no, seven years, I think."

"Seven is about it," Dave agreed. "And what concerns me is that in all that time, you still don't seem to have grasped what's really important to us."

Bob the Manager began to tense up. "I'm really sorry, but what have I missed exactly?"

"This is a fast-moving business, Bob. Technology advances not by the year, or month, or even week. We are on the fast track. My view is that things change daily. As the saying goes, 'The cheese has moved.' And it keeps moving at lightning speed."

"I *do* know that," Bob reassured his boss.

"If we're going to compete," Dave continued, "we have to remain keenly aware of what the competition is doing, and leap ahead of them."

"I know that, too, Dave."

"If that's the case, Bob, why are many of the forecasts you prepare delivered to my office late? Why is every budget turned in at the last possible moment? Why is 'just in time' inventory management such an ongoing struggle for your team? As Team Manager, you have the responsibility to make certain that essential events take place on time."

"Yes, I know, Dave. I assure you, I'm doing my best."

"Bob, last month you got two days behind in the delivery of motherboards to one of our biggest customers because you failed to order one little capacitor on time. That means our customer lost an entire day of production."

"I remember what happened exactly," Bob the Manager protested. "I was buried in paperwork at the time. Sometimes there just aren't enough hours in the day."

Dave wasn't buying Bob's excuse. "We just got word that we lost that account to Dyad Technologies. Seems they claim that they can deliver the boards on time. Apparently, their other customers are willing to back up that claim."

Bob the Manager turned red-faced. "I can't believe we lost that customer. I thought we were in solid with them. It was just one little slipup."

"This is business in today's world. According to the people in sales, your little slipup is going to cost our company almost $200,000 a year."

"I had no idea . . ."

"Well, now you do."

"In all my years here, I believe that's the only time I've blown a deadline, Dave. And it's certainly the first time we've ever lost any business because of me."

"It's not just the lost business, Bob. It's your whole pattern of just barely making deadlines. That pattern not only has impact on the quality of your work, but it causes delays in other departments. You always seem to come in right under the wire, and quite a bit of that shows in your work. You rush to get things done when time is running out, and you make mistakes. Some of them have been costly, whether you know it or not. We just can't tolerate that kind of sloppiness at Algalon. Your work habits are creating stress for your coworkers, and I'm almost certain you have to be feeling the stress yourself."

"You're right. I *am* stressed. But I've never thought of myself as a sloppy person," Bob said in his own defense.

"In some respects, it appears that you aren't. Every time I walk into your office, your desk is all organized and tidy. It's as though you focus on being 'Mr. Neat' rather than on the vital few aspects of your job."

"That's not true, Dave," Bob protested.

"The way I see it, Bob, you simply haven't determined what's important and what isn't. That's not working for me, nor will it work for Algalon or its customers."

"What are you saying, exactly?" Bob the Manager ventured with considerable hesitation.

"Bob, you're a good corporate citizen. You're one of the most likeable and generous guys in our company," Dave responded. "In fact, we all look up to you for reaching out to help others in the company and for your involvement in the community. While being a good match for our values is important, so are results. This is a business, and we have to operate it as such. All of the problems you've had lately are in your personnel file. It's all carefully documented. It's serious enough, Bob, that we're going to have to put you on probation."

Bob was completely taken aback. He had gone into this meeting thinking he might even be promoted. Now he was on probation! How could he have been so wrong?

Dave continued, "My friend, there are two things I look for in every key employee. They are *character* and *performance*. You are a person of great character. It's your performance that falls short. If you didn't possess character, you'd be out the door. I don't believe that character flaws can be easily corrected. But I do believe that performance issues can be resolved."

Bob breathed a silent sigh of relief and said, "I'm ready to work on it."

Dave's compassionate eyes revealed his true feelings toward Bob. "I want you to succeed, my friend. You have so much going for you. I don't want to have to let you go."

"Dave, I love Algalon. I've enjoyed my time here. What do I need to do to prove myself to you?"

"I have a new plan that might help you. When you get to the office, I want you to see the HR Director. She'll fill you in on the details."

"Will do," Bob assured his employer.

Dave offered a stern parting comment. "I hope you can change your ways, Bob . . . or you'll have to look for another opportunity. In today's business environment, companies simply can't afford to have any last-minute managers in their ranks."

TWO

Changes Ahead

Bob the Stunned Manager got into his car and drove to the office. He slowly walked down the seemingly endless corridor that led to the Human Resources Department. All the while, Dave's last words rang through his mind: ". . . companies simply can't afford to have any last-minute managers in their ranks."

I'm a competent manager, Bob thought. *I know this business inside and out. They need me here.*

Bob stepped into the HRD offices and waited for the Director to finish a phone call. He was escorted into her office and the door was closed.

"I'm sorry to hear that things aren't going well for you right now, Bob," the Director offered. "You've been here for quite some time. We all like you and would hate to see you go."

"I thought I'd be here forever," Bob admitted candidly.

The Director did what she could to offer encouragement. "Because Dave cares about people like you and wants good citizens also to be good performers, he has hired a new person in a brand-new position who will be able to help you become on-time and on-target. It's our belief that performance can be improved. In order to achieve that goal, you will have to go through The Process."

No mistake about it. Bob distinctly heard the capital letters in the phrase "The Process."

"What is 'The Process,' if I might ask?"

"Well, you will have to meet several times with the CEO and go through a certain process designed to—"

"The CEO?" Bob interrupted. "I have to meet with Dave? He's the one who sent me to meet with you."

The HR Director smiled. "I'm not talking about that CEO."

"Is there any other kind?" Bob wondered aloud.

"There is now. It's the Chief Effectiveness Officer."

Bob was mystified. "Chief Effectiveness Officer? I've never heard of such a thing." *Is Algalon becoming some kind of cult?* he questioned silently.

The HR Director continued, "The reason you've never heard of this position is probably because it was created just a few weeks ago."

"What exactly does this new kind of CEO do?" Bob queried.

"Our CEO's goal is to help good people like you improve performance by evaluating you in terms of the Three P's. Do you understand them? Do you apply them in your daily life at home and on the job? Are you willing to work on your performance challenges, or will you continue to be a last-minute manager?"

Spooky, Bob thought. *Dave used those same words: "last-minute manager."*

The HR Director went on, "You see, at Algalon, we are clearly seeing that our success is dependent upon every member of the team thinking and acting like an owner. If everyone is constantly looking farther up the hierarchy for decision-making, our customers will not be well served. So your ability to make key decisions on your own at crucial moments in time will be essential to our ongoing success. The Three P Strategy will empower you to meet that objective."

"What are the Three P's?" Bob asked.

"You'll find out when you meet with the CEO," the HR Director answered. "Are you free anytime tomorrow?"

"Yes. Early morning is best for me."

The HR Director dialed the CEO's extension and scheduled a meeting for Bob at 8 A.M. "I think Bob will benefit from The Process," the HR Director added. "He has the right heart but his performance record here is not up to par. We hope you can get him on track to being an on-time, on-target manager. That will probably involve giving him a checkup."

Bob couldn't help but wonder what the HR Director meant by that last comment. When the call ended, he asked, "Do I have to undergo a physical exam tomorrow?"

The HR Director chuckled. "No, not at all. It all has to do with your beliefs. You see, we have come to the conclusion that beliefs drive behavior, and if you're not getting the desired results, it can probably be traced to a lousy belief. The CEO will help you look at any flawed beliefs so you can become an on-time, on-purpose person. If she can do that, the chances for erasing this probation from your record will be outstanding."

Bob pondered her statements for a moment, then asked, "Do I need to do anything to prepare for the meeting? Should I bring anything with me?"

"No," replied the HR Director. "Just be on time."

• • •

When Bob got home, his wife looked at her husband's face and immediately sensed that something was wrong.

"I was put on probation," Bob confessed.

"You're not going to lose your job, are you?" she asked nervously.

"I don't think so . . . as long as I can become an on-time, on-target manager—as they refer to it."

"How do you do that?" Bob's wife asked.

"My understanding is that I have to schedule several meetings with the CEO."

"You're going to be meeting with Dave Pederson?"

Bob grinned. "Yeah, that's what I thought, too. The CEO I'll be meeting with is actually the Chief Effectiveness Officer."

"The Chief what?"

"Effectiveness Officer. I know, I know. I've never heard of that either. And I have only a vague understanding of what she does. It has something to do with reviewing my thinking—the beliefs I have."

Bob's wife was relieved. "It'll be a piece of cake, then. That's why I married you. I love your positive thinking. You always seem to stay upbeat."

"I hope I can this time, too," Bob said with a smile. "But there's some mystery involved. She's going to tell me all about the Three P's, and I have no idea what that means."

"You'll find out soon enough, I guess."

THREE

The First P

On the way to the office the following morning, with time to spare, Bob noticed that his gas gauge was hovering dangerously close to "E." *I don't know if I can make it,* he thought.

He pulled into the nearest gas station—the one that also appeared to have the longest waiting line he had seen in quite some time. He drummed his fingers impatiently as he waited for an elderly couple to pay for their gas and get a move on it.

At precisely 8:04 A.M., Bob the Perpetually Late Manager parked in his reserved space, dashed into the building, and headed straight for the CEO's office. He was greeted by a confident woman in her late twenties to mid-thirties.

"Good to meet you, Bob."

"Good to meet you, too," he responded warmly.

The CEO wasted no time getting to the point. "I'm sure you're wondering what a Chief Effectiveness Officer is."

"Took the words right out of my mouth," Bob admitted.

"This is a position Dave and I created. He was concerned about what he could do to help people become good performers. He always felt that if he had to choose between character and skills, he'd choose character. He felt that it's hard to teach people about values; skills should be easier to teach. I was interested in the same thing but realized that people with good hearts sometimes have their heads screwed on wrong—if you'll pardon the expression. While they may have servant hearts and good intentions, that is not reflected in their performance. People they have worked with over the years may have implanted some faulty thinking in their heads about serving customers and working with people. This faulty thinking prevents them from making significant contributions to the success of our business. As a result, their good character gets blocked in their head and never gets played out in performance.

"My job as CEO is to help our good people get in touch with what is really important, not only at work but in life, so they can help themselves and others win—and achieve the necessary goals."

Bob wasn't sure he wanted to ask the question that was on his mind, but he decided he had to. "Are you saying that we now practice some sort of religion here . . . and that I have to convert to it?"

The CEO smiled warmly. "No, it simply requires *reflection*. We want you to think deeply about who you are, why you want to be here, how you can contribute in greater ways, and how your being here will enrich your own life, our company's success, and our customers' satisfaction. It will become increasingly clear that our best people are those who understand who they are. That's because they take time to explore their thoughts, feelings, dreams, and goals. Ultimately, they come to realize that they can best achieve their goals—as well as those of our company—by becoming on-time, on-target individuals who make the most of the seconds, minutes, and hours that make up their days."

These are certainly things I've never really considered before, Bob thought as a clearly quizzical expression crossed his face.

The CEO continued. "This is the stuff of high principles, selfless actions, and life-changing attitudes. This is what will make our people and our company even more effective. You see, we firmly believe that the best companies first and foremost help their people become more than they ever aspired to be. Everyone who leaves our company for another should have more to offer their new employer than when they started here."

Bob was fascinated by this refreshing point of view . . . one that was completely new to the corporate culture. *Dave may have made a really good decision with this CEO thing.*

"Second, the best companies serve their customers by delivering exactly what they promise—and even more than promised. On time, at the agreed-upon price. Customers want what they want, when and where they want it, with high quality at a fair price. These are the principles we use to develop loyalty, even when economic conditions are challenging."

She continued, "Third, the best companies help ensure their vendors' survival. A supplier that isn't profitable may not be around to help us meet our own objectives in the future. Of course we want the best prices on raw materials. But we don't want to beat up our vendors. We want them to make a fair profit. And we strive to pay them within their terms, rather than the terms we would likely prefer to set on our own."

"So the reason I've been put on probation rather than being fired is to see if I can get and adopt this positive philosophy?" Bob ventured.

"That's it, Bob. The company has invested a lot in you over the years. That makes you valuable here. I'm sure you realize that we're not in business to meet just short-term goals. We're in this for the long haul. We want our company to survive—and to thrive—because then everyone wins on an ongoing basis. We can only secure our future by meeting our customers' needs; by enlisting the support of our vendors; by treating one another with respect, fairness, and honesty; and by building an internal team of on-time achievers. We don't want any last-minute managers in this company. If we achieve that goal, we won't have any last-minute employees, either."

This has to be some sort of conspiracy, Bob thought to himself as he digested the phrase "last-minute manager" yet another time.

"What do I have to do to help the company reach its objectives?" Bob asked with deep sincerity.

"Very simply, Bob, it's best if all of us who work here understand and subscribe to what I call the 'Three P Strategy.'"

"Our HR Director mentioned the Three P thing, but I admit I have no idea what she meant by it."

"It's really straightforward, Bob. As you know, we are a player in a fast-moving industry. We don't travel in the slow lane. To avoid being a last-minute company, we have to be in the right place at the right time with the right solutions. For that reason, we have to make certain that everyone in our company is on the same team, playing the same game. Anyone who doesn't make decisions based on the Three P's is going to hurt us more than he or she helps us."

Bob's curiosity was increasingly piqued. "What are the Three P's?"

The CEO paused for a moment. "I'm sorry, but I can't really answer that question."

Bob the Bewildered Manager sat there in utter silence, completely puzzled.

The CEO laughed. "I'm not trying to play games with you. What I mean is that understanding the Three P's is a process, not merely a list or an answer to a question. We'll take one step at a time."

"You're going to tell me what the first P is then?"

"I sure am."

The CEO pushed a small button on her desk and the office became a whirlwind of technological activity. The lights dimmed, a projection screen dropped out of the ceiling, eerie music played from all directions, and a video projector flashed a brilliant image onto the screen. The image was a single word that moved and danced, surrounded by a glowing halo effect. The word was **"Priority."** Suddenly, accompanied by stunning sound effects, the word appeared to be burned and chiseled into a stone tablet.

I had no idea we had this kind of high-tech stuff here, Bob the Skeptical Manager thought. *I thought we were still in the world of whiteboards, Post-it notes, and big tablets of paper on easels.*

As quickly as it had all happened, the image disappeared, the music faded out, the screen retracted, and the lights came back on.

"That's it?" Bob asked. "The first P is 'Priority'?"

"That's it! Impressive, huh?"

"I doubt that I'll ever forget it," Bob admitted with a sly grin.

"That's the whole idea," the CEO confirmed. "The people who work here need to understand their priorities. They can never, ever forget them."

"So what are they?" Bob asked.

The CEO reached into her left desk drawer, pulled out a nine-by-twelve-inch envelope, and handed it to him.

"This is your homework for tonight. After dinner, find someplace quiet and complete this questionnaire. Then bring it back to me tomorrow, same time."

"If I answer the questions correctly, will I be taken off probation?" Bob asked candidly.

"There aren't really any right or wrong answers, Bob. There are only *your* answers," the CEO declared as she rose to her feet, obviously signaling the end of the meeting.

Bob tucked the envelope under his arm, stood up, and shook hands with the CEO. "I'll see you tomorrow."

FOUR

The First Test

When Bob the Last-Minute Manager got home, his wife told him that the kids were "really in the mood for pizza," so they ordered the largest one available—the stuffed-crust variety with lots of toppings.

Bob's wife wanted to hear about every detail of his day. "How did your session with the Chief Whatever go today?" she asked between her first and second slices of pizza.

"Cthief Effectiveneth Offither," Bob replied, his mouth full of mozzarella. "It went really fine, I guesth."

"What do you mean by that?"

Bob swallowed and responded, "She seems like a sincere person. I mean, she really cares about the company and all of us employees. But there are so many things about 'The Process' that I don't understand."

"For example . . . ?"

"Okay, for example, she told me about the first P—Priority—and handed me a sealed envelope. It's some kind of test, apparently, and I have to find a quiet place after dinner to fill it out."

"*Very* unusual," Bob's wife agreed. "But didn't you tell me there are three P's? How about the other two?"

"I have no idea. I guess she'll tell me tomorrow."

Bob helped clean up after dinner, and when the kids had finally shuffled off to bed, he settled behind his desk in the study. He opened the envelope expecting to find a lengthy test comprised of perhaps dozens of probing questions. Instead, he pulled out a single sheet of paper that, along with a place to write his name and the date, bore exactly two questions.

1. Please rank the following personal and business priorities in order by placing numbers from 1 to 7 in front of them (1 being the most important).

   _____ Health and Fitness

   _____ Faith/Spiritual Life

   _____ Career

   _____ Spouse and/or Family

_____ Friends

_____ Education/Knowledge

_____ Recreation/Sports

Bob studied the list for the longest time. *Do I prioritize them according to how I think the CEO wants me to, or according to what I really believe?* he wondered.

He thought some more. *I suppose I should list career first and family second. Need the career to support the family, right?*

After considerable rehashing, Bob eventually settled on his priorities, placing "Recreation/Sports" in sixth place, just a nick above "Faith/Spiritual Life," which finished dead last. *I suppose this could be a huge mistake, since I got a sense, in an offhanded sort of way that she is a spiritual person . . .*

Bob moved on to the second question. This one seemed even more bizarre than the first.

2. Please rank these events according to their priority in your life today. In other words, which one of these responsibilities would rise to the top of your "to do" list, assuming they were all on your list at the same time?

_____ A personal doctor's appointment you've had for three weeks

_____ Your child's (or niece's or nephew's) game, concert, or recital

_____ A family health emergency

_____ A meeting scheduled at the request of your employer

_____ An appointment with an important customer

_____ A long-planned evening out with friends

_____ A "date" with your spouse or significant person

Bob had long believed that "work comes first," and that his primary allegiance had to be to his employer, so he ranked the meeting with his employer and the appointment with an important customer ahead of a long-planned evening out with friends and a date with his spouse. He struggled more with the child's game, concert, or recital and the illness of a family member. *Right up there in importance,* he thought. The "no-brainer" on this list was the personal doctor's appointment. *That could wait. After all, he always makes* me *wait!*

When Bob had finished, he noticed one last instruction on the page:

> Before returning this questionnaire, please look up the word "Priority" in your dictionary.

I probably should have done this first, he said to himself as he pulled the dictionary from the bookshelf and began to flip through the pages. On page 1131, he read this definition:

> **pri-or-i-ty**
>
> (1) being earlier or more important, precedence in rank or order, the right to be first; (2) something that is more important than other items or considerations.

That's pretty much what I thought. Bob made a mental note of the definition, returned the dictionary to the shelf, and stuffed the questionnaire back into the envelope.

As he climbed into his bed hoping for a good night's sleep, an uneasy thought drifted in and out of his mind. *What if she doesn't like my answers?*

FIVE

Denial

Bob the Last-Minute Manager was almost late for his scheduled appointment with the CEO. But, in his mind, there was a perfectly good reason why he had to make a mad dash for her office and why he arrived out of breath. His mother had called. When she heard he'd been put on probation she reminded him that if he had gone into medicine as she had suggested—no, *pleaded*—he would have been much more successful. "Doctors make so much more money than engineers who become managers," she chided. "You should have listened to your mother."

Thankfully, the CEO didn't seem to notice that Bob was gasping for air. She invited him to take a seat and got right down to business. "Bob, I believe there are three fatal traits of last-minute managers. They are common to all procrastinators, but they aren't necessarily the result of procrastination. They are more often than not the actual cause."

Hearing the words "last-minute manager" again, Bob took a deep but solemn breath, fearful that the CEO was going to pinpoint some of his faults.

"First," the CEO continued, "procrastinators delay taking action regarding their priorities. They keep busy, but often on the wrong things. They put off action on important things. As a result, the high priority items are often delayed. It becomes a lateness issue."

"I see," Bob said, unable to look her in the eye.

"Second, even when they do get to the point of establishing their priorities, they jump from one task to another, believing that it's important to keep all the balls in the air at the same time. Eventually, they complain about having too many 'loose ends' to tie up. That becomes a quality-of-work problem.

"Finally, whether procrastinators want to admit it or not, they cause stress for themselves and others. They cause stress for themselves because they run around and try to get things done at the last moment. They cause stress for others who are forced to worry about deadlines to bail out the procrastinator."

"So the issues for procrastinators are lateness, poor quality work, and causing stress for themselves and others," Bob interjected.

"That's it exactly," said the CEO. "Priority—the first P—has the biggest impact on lateness. With that in mind, did you finish your assignment?" she asked.

"I did," he replied as he handed her the questionnaire. "I was surprised that there were only two questions, though."

The CEO said nothing as she reviewed Bob's answers. He waited . . . and waited. After a few moments, the CEO put the paper down and smiled.

"Tell me," he asked hesitantly, "did I get my priorities in order?"

"As I told you yesterday, there are no right or wrong answers. Priorities are constantly shifting. It's impossible to make a list and have it stand for all time. The list is going to change."

"Please explain what you mean."

"Have you ever been to the emergency room in a hospital?"

"Yes, I have." Bob replied. "Our son, Jared, broke his arm sliding into the catcher at home plate last year. We spent hours just sitting around in the emergency room before anyone saw him. It was far from the most pleasant experience."

The CEO empathized. "Broken arms don't count for much, do they?"

"They sure don't," Bob agreed.

"The explanation behind your long wait is the triage nurse, of course."

"I've heard the term 'triage' before, but I've never bothered to find out exactly what it means."

"It's a term that originated in the battlefield setting. It's basically a system of assigning priorities for medical treatment of casualties on the basis of urgency, the severity of the wounds, and the patient's chances for survival. So in the ER, chances are every automobile accident victim came ahead of your son's broken arm."

"That's true. But what does that have to do with business?"

"We're going to expect everyone at Algalon to 'triage' every activity. That way, they'll always handle the important things—the priorities—first, instead of dealing with things on a first-come, first-served basis. People who know what's most important are seldom late when dealing with these high priorities."

Bob responded with an expression that said, "Tell me more."

The CEO pointed to a chart on the wall.

Yes	**Maybe**	**No**
Want to do and have to do	**Want to do but don't have to do**	**Don't want to do and don't have to do**
Have to do but don't want to do		

"As you can see, there are four categories of daily activities that we all face.

- The things we **want** to do and **have** to do;
- The things we **have** to do but **don't want** to do;
- The things we **want** to do but **don't have** to do;
- The things we **don't want** to do and **don't have** to do.

"The first two are in the 'Yes' column. The third is in the 'Maybe' column. The fourth is in the 'No' column. The worst of the last-minute managers actually perform some of the tasks in the 'No' column. That's a tragedy!"

"I can see how that would be true," Bob agreed.

The CEO continued, "It's easy to do the 'want to and have to' tasks. It's easy, too, to do the 'want to but don't have to' tasks, because they are personally rewarding. There's a 'want to but don't have to' item on my list today. I'd love to go golfing. But if I were to do that, it would interfere with the 'have to' items on my list."

"That makes sense to me," Bob agreed . . . while reflecting on the many times he had gotten this out of order.

"Bob, I noticed that in your answer to the first question, 'health and fitness' were more than halfway down the list. That may be a 'have to do but don't want to do' item for you."

"You could be right. I have always thought of repetitive exercise as being boring, although lately I've gotten more enthusiastic about my visits to the club. Also, I find my days go better if I have an early morning walk. So exercise seems to be moving to the 'want to do and have to do' category. It's exhilarating, and I sleep better, too."

"That's great," the CEO acknowledged. "But in answer to the second question, you indicated that an appointment with your doctor would be at the bottom of your list."

"Yeah, I believe that's how I answered."

"If you're generally in good health, I can understand why you might blow off an appointment with your doctor in favor of a social event or a meeting with a client."

"Well, I *am* in pretty good health."

"That's good to know. But let's say that your appointment with your doctor was to verify that your chemotherapy treatments had successfully eradicated cancer from your body. What then?"

Bob answered without hesitation. "My appointment with my doctor would probably be the most important event on my calendar. It would be a 'want to and have to.'"

"Right! Another example: Your social evening out is with friends who are moving to New Zealand the next day and it could be years before you see them again."

"That would move up on my list, too."

"So the point is that situations—your knowledge of the existing circumstances—dictate your priorities."

"I guess so."

"Our goal is to make certain that everyone who works here understands that priorities change. Our guiding principle is that we must *know what to do and when to do it.*"

"Can you explain that?"

"Okay, I'll do the best I can. People often create meaningless tasks for themselves, and then allow those tasks to move to the top of their priority list. Worse yet, they will let others create meaningless tasks for them. If you are able to develop an open, candid relationship with your supervisor—something we are going to strongly encourage in our company—you will be in a position to question assignments that don't appear to be true priorities. Then the two of you agree to 'triage' them, and delete them from the list of assignments."

"Does that mean there are actually some things that I shouldn't do at all?"

"Exactly. Here's a personal example. In my last position, I thought that one of the most important aspects of my job was to read all of the trade journals that crossed my desk. I was, in effect, creating meaningless tasks for myself. Finally, it occurred to me that I was so consumed with reading this mountain of material that I was ignoring the more important tasks."

"Ouch! I've done that myself," Bob admitted sheepishly. "In retrospect, after flipping through hundreds of pages, I seldom learned anything all that useful. But at least I could scratch 'read industry magazines' off my list."

The CEO laughed. "I'm sure there are useful things in many of the publications, but if the ideas are all that earthshaking, they'll eventually come to the surface anyway. I eventually canceled subscriptions to the least relevant publications, or passed them on to other people who could better utilize the information."

Bob nodded his head in agreement. "I thought I would be more valuable to Algalon if I acquired volumes of knowledge from as many sources as possible, so that's why I read all of those magazines. But my job isn't to glean all of that information, it's to manage a production process."

The CEO nodded. "A lot of managers believe that *activity* translates into *productivity*—and that *productivity* translates into *results.* So they create long to do lists filled with activities. Then they complete all of those activities and, after they do, they believe that they've been productive. When they eventually discover that there are no meaningful results, they are mystified. After all, they've been busy. They've crossed things off their lists. In the meantime, the important tasks have been ignored and they haven't delegated a single thing. They haven't triaged their activities. They have become last-minute managers by default. It's all a form of denial, really."

"Denial?" Bob asked.

"Bob, do you know what the number one killer of adults in America is?"

Bob thought for a moment. "Cancer, I imagine."

"Good answer. But try again."

"Heart attacks?"

"Another possibility. Do you have another guess?"

"Strokes?"

"Could be."

"I give up."

A pained look crossed the CEO's face. "I personally believe that the number one killer is denial."

"Denial?" Bob asked as he considered her statement.

"Yes," the CEO replied, tears building in her eyes. "We just talked about how important your appointment with your doctor would be to you if its purpose were to check up on the progress of your cancer treatments. . . ."

"That's right," Bob acknowledged.

The CEO struggled to continue. "My dad died of denial. For more than two years, he experienced severe pains in his abdomen. He even wrote about it in his journal. My mom discovered the horrible truth almost three years after he died—when she read what he had written. When it came to his health, my dad was a last-minute manager. He didn't know how to prioritize. So instead of going in for regular colon exams for early detection of cancer, he went into denial. He visited his doctor too late. As a result, he endured four drawn-out surgeries, ten weeks in the hospital, and two months in a nursing home. Then he died. Of denial. Not of cancer. But of his last-minute solutions to a dire situation."

The CEO wiped her tears away. "I'm sorry. I shouldn't tell you this kind of heavy stuff in our sessions."

Compassion overtook Bob. "That's all right," he said. "I'm sorry about your dad. He must have been very special to you."

"He was. He never missed one of my soccer games. He never missed a piano recital. But he missed my graduation from grade school to junior high. He died two weeks before it—at the last minute. And I still really miss him. I miss him so much."

Bob and the CEO were silent for an uncomfortably long time.

Finally, the CEO spoke. "So Priority emphasizes triaging and making sure that what's most important gets your immediate attention. That helps last-minute managers overcome their lateness tendency."

"What about the other two traits—poor quality work and stress creators?"

The CEO smiled. "Remember, we have two more P's to go!"

SIX

The Second P

"Bob, the good news is, there is a way—that's powerful and effective—to decide among the various options that confront us. There is a way to know what to do and when to do it. There's a way to get our priorities in order. That's the secret of the second P."

The CEO pushed her magic button and again the lights dimmed. The projection screen dropped, ethereal music began to play, and a single word flashed onto the screen. It quickly exploded to life and, accompanied by sound effects, was chiseled onto a stone tablet.

I'm beginning to detect a pattern here, Bob decided as the word became etched in stone.

"Propriety."

"That's the second P," the CEO announced with a healthy dose of pride. "Any questions?"

Bob hesitated. "Only one. What does it mean?"

"Do you want my definition . . . or Webster's?"

"Let's start with Webster's."

The CEO didn't have to look it up in the dictionary. This definition was solidly embedded in her mind. "There are three components. First, it means 'the quality or state of being proper or suitable.' Second, it means 'correctness of behavior or morals.' Finally, it means 'conformity with accepted standards.'"

"That's pretty much what I thought it meant, but I have to tell you something candidly. I don't think I've used that word in years. Maybe I've never used it. It seems so old-fashioned. Out-of-date. Prudish. Like something from the Victorian era."

Through her laughter, the CEO admitted, "You're right, Bob. It *is* old-fashioned. I can't remember my parents using the word even once as I was growing up. But I can't think of one other word—let alone a 'P' word—that means exactly what 'propriety' means. The word itself may be kind of snooty and out-of-date, but the concepts it represents are very current and extremely vital."

Bob pondered her words, then suggested, "I imagine there's some kind of test that goes along with this."

"Actually, no. But I do have a little handout for you to contemplate when you get home." The CEO gave Bob another nine-by-twelve envelope. "This is our company's brand-new 'Bill of Rights.' There are seven points. They define what 'propriety' will mean to us from now on. And every on-time, on-target manager in our company will adhere to them strictly in order to be successful and produce high quality work. Study them tonight, and tomorrow we'll talk about them. Same time, okay?"

"Sounds great! I'll be here," Bob said. But as he packed up his computer and PDA at the end of the day, he thought, *I wonder if there's any chance everyone in this company is going to buy into this program.*

SEVEN

The "Bill of Rights"

Bob was so stressed out from his second session with the CEO that he decided to stop at the health club on his way home—something he was beginning to do a bit more frequently, despite his dislike of rigid exercise routines. Once on the road, he called his wife from his cell phone to make sure she concurred with his plans. There was no answer, so he left a message for her.

He did a full routine, nearly burning himself out, then enjoyed an extraordinarily long respite in the spa and the steam room. He watched CNN on the locker-room TV as he dressed. *Maybe the spa, the steam room, and CNN are the reasons I'm finally getting more into the health club routine,* he told himself.

Then—as refreshed and relaxed as he'd been in days—he drove home at a full ten miles per hour below the speed limit. Unusual behavior for Always-in-a-Hurry Bob.

He arrived to an empty house. No wife. No daughter. No son. *Where had they all headed off to?* He was just settling in to watch the fourth quarter of an NBA game when his family walked in.

"Dad, where were you?" his daughter demanded—half screaming, half in tears—as she stormed off to her room.

"Yeah, Dad. Good job," Bob's son added as he grabbed a slice of cold pizza from the fridge and headed toward his room. "We were all wondering where you were. You promised you'd be there."

Bob was suddenly alone—except for the chilling fact that his disgruntled wife was still within striking distance. "Okay, Bob, I want to know something. Don't you ever look at that fancy, expensive electronic calendar of yours? How could you forget something as important as Michelle's line dance competition?"

"That was tonight?" Bob the Completely Out-of-Touch Manager asked.

"Yes, Bob. It was tonight. Somehow it didn't make your dandy new priority list. You seem to participate in everything at the last minute—if at all!"

Those words burned bitterly in Bob's mind as his wife angrily ascended the stairs to their bedroom. Her last audible words were, "I am sure disappointed in you, Robert. And so are your children."

Bob sat there for the longest time as he agonized over his wife's parting comments. Countless thoughts poured through his mind.

Am I that bad a husband?

Am I that awful a father?

Am I an undesirable employee?

Am I really a Last-Minute Manager?

Bob was immersed in his thoughts and deep in remorse when his wife quietly came back down the stairs and slipped into the family room.

"I'm sorry, Bob. I shouldn't have been so hard on you, but Michelle was excited that you were going to come to her line dance competition and when you didn't show, she was really hurt."

"I'm the one who should be saying 'I'm sorry,'" said Bob. "I feel like a complete failure."

"You're not a failure, Bob," she responded as she wrapped her arms around him. "You're just—we're just—going through a lot right now. And this so-called Chief Effectiveness Officer isn't making things any easier."

"I'm not so sure about that," Bob suggested. "I think she may be helping me see things in a different light, even though it didn't help tonight. In fact, today I got another mystery envelope. I'm going to get through it, no matter what. I don't care how unusual this whole process is, I'm going to stick with it to the end. I'm going to get taken off probation. And, blast it, from now on, I'm not going to be known as a last-minute manager!"

Bob headed for the study. He opened the envelope and pulled out a single sheet of paper. There were no questions to answer. Just a short list of thoughts to consider.

PROPRIETY: THE BILL OF RIGHTS

- Do the right thing.
- Do it for the right reasons.
- Do it with the right people.
- Do it at the right time.
- Do it in the right order.
- Do it with intensity.
- Do it for the right results.

Bob studied the words, then studied them some more. He thought about the events that had just taken place that evening.

If this means what I think it does, I violated the rights of my family in a big way tonight. I sure didn't do the right thing. The right thing would have been to attend Michelle's competition. I could've been there if I had just taken ten seconds to check my schedule. The right reason is because she's my daughter and she wants me to see her perform. The right people? Well, that would be my family. There's no question that I did everything at the wrong time in the wrong order for the wrong results. I think I need to apologize—and do it with intensity.

Bob stuffed the sheet of paper back into the envelope and went to find his daughter. He took her in his arms and said, "Michelle, I can't begin to tell you how sorry I am that I missed your competition. I just blew it. I have no excuse. I don't know how I can make it up to you but I'll try. I promise you one thing, though. You're going to see some changes in my behavior. I want to be a part of your life and be a dad you can love and be proud of."

Michelle looked up at him with tears in her eyes. "Thanks, Dad."

The world is suddenly a better place, Bob thought as he headed down the hall to his son's room to finish the night's apologies. When he finally climbed into bed with his wife, they didn't say anything, but just hugged each other.

• • •

Bob the More Determined Manager actually showed up for his appointment with the CEO five minutes early. *I hope she notices!* She didn't. Or if she did, she didn't acknowledge it.

"What do you think about the second P?" she asked.

"I personally discovered last night that 'propriety' not only helps us determine what our priorities should be, but also what needs to be done to ensure that what we do is high quality," Bob said confidently.

"You're right. That's exactly it."

"I imagine it will take some time and practice for me to be able to apply the Bill of Rights to all of my priorities on a consistent basis."

"It will," the CEO agreed. "But if you stick with me, you'll discover that I've found some unique ways to help you with that."

"What ways?"

"Here's a simple example: I'm going to begin to deliver a daily voicemail message for interested employees. Anyone in the company will have the option of dialing a special extension to listen to it. I've researched all sorts of little nuggets of time-tested, life-changing wisdom from a variety of sources, and I will be sharing them in those brief messages."

"Do you have an example of these nuggets?" Bob the Still Somewhat Skeptical Manager asked.

"Sure. Here's one you've heard, I imagine. 'What a person plants, he or she will harvest.'"

"I've heard that. 'As you sow, so shall you reap,' right?"

"That's it. Of course, this is not simply about corn or beans or wheat. It's about life in general. If parents don't spend time with their kids when they're young—teaching them right from wrong and listening to their thoughts and dreams—they can't expect to have good relationships with them later in life. They can't count on their kids to make sound decisions, either. So that's a priority."

"That makes sense," Bob the Still Feeling Guilty Father said. "And I guess you could say that particular thought is time-tested."

"How about this thought? 'Two wrongs don't make a right.'"

"I've heard that one, too."

"As true as that seems to be, we have a twist on that saying, based on the Bill of Rights. 'Two rights don't make a wrong.' No matter what decision is facing you, if you can apply two or more of the 'rights' to the situation, you'll seldom go wrong. The more rights you bring to the situation, the better the outcome will likely be."

"Interesting thought," said Bob.

"Here's another one: 'Treat others the way you would like to be treated.'"

Bob jumped right in again. "You mentioned that one the first day we met. 'Do unto others as you would have them do unto you.'"

"Right again. The point is, that's one of the time-tested truths that serves as a guideline for how our company intends to conduct business now and in the future. Far too many businesses operate under the principle 'Do *others* in before they do *you* in.'"

"That's the truth," Bob agreed.

"In our company, our long-term goal is to do our best to make sure that everyone comes out ahead—our customers, our suppliers, our coworkers, and, yes, even our managers and upper-level executives. Our new goal will be to make certain that we never have a labor-management conflict again. Our people need to trust management—and vice versa."

"That's an impressive goal!" Bob the Impressed Manager exclaimed.

"Not so impressive when we understand what our priorities are, and how the principles of propriety mesh with them."

"Still, our company has never thought this way before. I guess that's why I'm amazed."

"As you can probably guess, most of my morning phone messages will apply my nuggets of wisdom to the Three P's and the Bill of Rights."

"I assume you have specific definitions for all of the points on the Bill of Rights, then," Bob supposed.

"I do, but I'm hoping that you'll give me your definitions."

Bob eagerly agreed to take on this latest assignment.

"What do you imagine we mean by **'Do the right thing'**?" the CEO asked.

"I'd guess you mean that there's right and wrong, and you want our people to choose what's right over what's wrong," Bob suggested.

"We sure do. But how do you know what's 'right' and what's 'wrong'?"

"You got me there," Bob confessed. "Instincts, maybe?"

"Good instincts help, but I like to use what's become known as The Ethics Check," said the CEO. "When confronted by a potential ethical problem—where right and wrong may be at odds—I ask myself three questions:

1. ***Is it legal?***
   Will I be violating either civil law or company policy?

2. ***Is it balanced?***
   Is it fair to all concerned in the short term as well as in the long term? Does it promote win-win relationships?

3. ***How will it make me feel about myself?***
   Will it make me proud?
   Would I feel good if my decision were to be published in the newspaper?
   Would I feel good if my family knew about it?

"The first question is about legality, the second about fairness, and the third involves self-esteem. Most people only ask the legal question. But there are times when something may be legal but not ethical."

"Can you give me an example?"

"Sure," the CEO replied. "We've all read about examples where something was legal in terms of accounting procedures, but unfair to coworkers, customers, and stockholders. If the top managers knew that what they did was going to be made public, they probably would have thought twice about it."

Bob reflected on her words for a moment. "You're right. Just because something is legal doesn't make it right. You have to ask all three questions. That's powerful."

"I think so," said the CEO with a smile. "But the next principle—do it for the right reasons—is a bit more tricky."

"What do you mean 'tricky'?"

"It has to do with motives. Think about Martin Luther King, Jr., for example. He did the right thing. He worked for civil rights. But did he do it for personal fame? Did he do it to make money? Or did he do it to help millions of people attain equality?"

"For equality," Bob quickly replied.

"Right! Although he never made a fortune as the result of his efforts, he did achieve a measure of fame. But that was merely a by-product of his efforts to erase the boundaries of race and color. His goal was—according to The Ethics Check motto—to 'promote win-win relationships.'"

"Yet he died from an assassin's bullet," Bob observed.

"True. Doing the right thing for the right reasons offers no assurance of personal safety or freedom from pain. Last-minute managers often do everything possible to avoid personal pain, but true leaders do what needs to be done to alleviate the pain of others."

"So do you really think that Martin Luther King, Jr., was willing to die for his cause?"

"I'd guess that he never imagined he would die in the way he did, but I believe he knew that his cause was just and that he would have an enduring impact."

"How does this all relate to **'Do it with the right people'**?"

The CEO thought for a moment. "I believe that when it comes to working with others, there are two levels of interaction—form and essence. Form involves the kinds of work you do together and how you do that work. Essence operates on a deeper level: 'heart to heart' and 'values to values.'

"To me, essence comes before form. I need to know who people are before I decide to do something with them. I prefer to do things—whether they are business assignments or social events—with other people who practice the Three P's. For example, if I were to form a partnership with someone who didn't share my values and want to do the right thing, I could open myself up to a lot of conflict. I'd rather work with people who keep their word and can be trusted. If I tell someone something in confidence I don't want to read it the next day in an e-mail sent out to the entire company."

Bob grasped her point immediately. "My daughter told something to her best friend in confidence, and her friend spread it all over school. She was heartbroken."

"It's a tough lesson for anyone to learn," the CEO agreed. "And the reality is, even the best managers can't always pick the right people. But we can avoid the most obvious mistakes. We don't go to our automobile mechanic to diagnose health problems, and we don't ask our doctors to tune up our engines."

Bob laughed. "You're right."

"The same principle applies in organizations. Last-minute managers do not make good partners."

Bob the Feeling-Guilty-as-Charged Manager swallowed the lump in his throat and asked, "Um . . . what's next?"

"The next 'do it,' of course, is **'Do it at the right time.'** This all gets back to the whole issue of 'Priority.' There's a time to meet with clients. There's a time to see your doctor if you have a health concern. Since you can't possibly do everything at the same time, part of setting your priorities and producing high quality work is doing things at the right time.

"A rock band my dad used to listen to—the Byrds—did a song written by Pete Seeger called 'Turn, Turn, Turn.' The lyrics were:

"'To everything . . . turn, turn, turn . . .
There is a season . . . turn, turn, turn . . .
And a time to every purpose under heaven.

A time to be born, a time to die.
A time to plant, a time to reap.
A time to laugh, a time to weep.'"

"I love that old song!" Bob said with a smile.

The CEO continued, "Knowing 'what time it is' is important. If I want to have a child, when should I be thinking about that? When I'm thirty? Or when I'm seventy?"

"When you're thirty, of course."

"Right! And if our company is to sustain our success, all of our managers have to be keenly aware of timing. Sometimes it's not just being on time. There is often a need to be early. A last-minute manager may meet the deadline, but the truly effective person often achieves the objectives ahead of schedule, so that the results can be tweaked—and even perfected."

"So you're saying that adding a cushion of time offers the opportunity to do 'more, better, faster, differently,' and with less chance for error?"

"You've got it, Bob! Our most productive people will need to understand that some things have to happen before other things can—or should—happen. They will **'Do it in the right order.'**"

"First things first, in other words?" Bob posed.

"Exactly," the CEO agreed. "A builder doesn't put the roof on a house until the walls are up, and the walls can't go up before the foundation is poured. The foundation can't be poured before the ground is leveled, and the ground can't be leveled until the surveyors have done their work. And the surveyors have to rely on the blueprints for the house to get all of the elevations correct. Can't have rainwater flowing down the driveway into the garage."

"I understand. I watched all of that take place when we had our new house built a few years ago," Bob concurred.

"It's clear, then, that the first step is always the plan—the blueprint. It's impossible to build a house without a plan, just as it's impossible to build a company without a plan. In our case, our plan will be our 'Mission Statement'—our reason for being. I believe that last-minute managers either fail to understand the vision, or they lose sight of it. On-time, on-target managers are always guided by the vision."

"I'm afraid the 'vision' thing doesn't do much for me," Bob confessed.

"What do you mean exactly?" the CEO asked.

"I think that we have a hokey, overblown mission statement that essentially means nothing. It says something like, 'Our mission is to be the leading supplier in our market niche by providing technically innovative products and stellar personal service to our customers in a timely manner.'"

"I know what you're saying," the CEO agreed. "Sometimes I think that the people who write these things simply compile long strings of lofty-sounding words and call them mission statements."

"That's why people have difficulty buying into them, I think," Bob said.

"Are you saying, 'The simpler the better'?"

"Yes, that's it."

"I have a perfect example for you, then. The Phoenix, Arizona, Fire Department is one of the most highly regarded fire departments in the nation. It has 1,549 employees who respond to approximately 128,000 calls a year, yet zero employee grievances a year is the norm, and two grievances is considered a flood."

"That's unheard of," said Bob. "How do they pull that off?"

"A relative of mine works for the department. He told me about the fire chief, Alan Brunacini, who has been the head of the department for well over two decades. One of the first things he did when he stepped into the position was to trim the hundreds of rules down to a few essentials that fit on a single sheet of paper. Another key action was to give each employee a card that offered seven guidelines for firefighter empowerment, along with eight essentials of customer service."

"Customer service? What's that all about?" Bob wondered.

"Chief Brunacini has communicated to his people that they are there to serve people—not just save buildings."

"That sure seems like a sound philosophy," Bob observed.

"The chief's most important decisions were to steer his department away from a punitive environment—the 'it's my way or the highway' attitude—and to 'walk the talk.' The members of the leadership team were coached to live the principles they espoused."

"They had to practice what they preached, right?"

"Right."

"What does all this have to do with mission?"

"What the chief did, Bob, was essentially distill the mission of his department down to five simple words: 'Prevent harm, survive, be nice.'"

"That's their mission statement? That's it?"

The CEO smiled. "In a nutshell. But don't you see what's behind it? It encompasses much of the Three P Strategy. The priorities are clear. 'Prevent harm' is the first priority. 'Survive' is right behind that. And 'be nice' is crucial to customer service. It's all there in five words."

All Bob could say in reply was, "Amazing!"

The CEO continued. "Those five words also say something about propriety. The Phoenix firefighters are doing the right thing—preventing harm—for the right reasons—saving lives. They are also doing it with the right people—their comrades who share in the vision and who also seek to prevent harm. Obviously, they're doing it at the right time, but they also do it all in the right order. Their equipment is maintained properly so that it can help them perform on the job. When they respond to a fire call, they deploy the equipment properly—they use it to save lives first and save buildings second. Ladders before hoses."

"That's a great mission statement for a fire department," Bob admitted. "But why is ours so lame?"

"I'm glad you asked that question, Bob. Because we're going to develop a vision for our company, one that not only has a clear purpose or mission statement, but also tells us where we're going—our picture of the future—and what's going to guide our journey—our values. And you're going to be a part of it."

"What do you mean?"

"As you implied, Bob, when the vision is unclear—or fuzzy—the results are fuzzy. People tend to procrastinate when they don't have a clear picture of who they are, where they are at this moment, and where they want to go. After all, if they don't know where they're going, they have no clue whether the next action they take—the next activity they engage in—will help take them there."

"I think I understand," Bob ventured. "Why do something unless you are clear what the outcome will be? In that case, I think I'd do something else."

"Right!" the CEO agreed, obviously pleased with what she had heard. "On the job, the top priority should be to accomplish those tasks that contribute to the vision. Because there's a limit to the number of available hours in a day, some things that do not contribute to the vision—including all those magazines we talked about yesterday—will have to be 'triaged' off the agenda."

"So you're saying that we will have a clearly defined vision for our company?" Bob the Finally-Starting-to-Get-It Manager wondered.

"We sure will. Every employee will be involved in its creation, so that everyone has an opportunity to buy into it. A compelling vision will be grounded on our past but focused on our future. So the purpose of everything we do in the present will be designed to lead us into tomorrow. Our vision will be very straightforward and we will express it in simple terms. It will help us know *who* we are, *why* we are here, and *where* we are going. We know there will be fires in our future, so we know we have to be properly equipped to extinguish them."

"Makes sense to me. But I'm eager to learn more about the other points on your 'Bill of Rights' list, and I'd sure like to know how they all fit together."

The CEO smiled. "Bob, I like your enthusiasm for what we're doing here."

Bob laughed. "I have to be enthusiastic. This is about my job, remember?"

The CEO smiled and said, "The next one, as you'll recall, is **'Do it with intensity.'**"

"By that, you must mean 'Put your heart into it,'" Bob the Winging-It Manager suggested.

"Right again! Intensity is part enthusiasm, part passion, part skill, and part unwavering devotion. Think about great basketball stars, outstanding Olympic athletes, or champion golfers or tennis players. A loss—a setback—never diminishes their intensity. Because they are enthusiastic, passionate, well trained, and devoted, they are not set back by setbacks. They can take a huge blow and get right back in the game. The players who lack intensity drop out when they confront obstacles."

Bob thought for a minute. "What you're saying, I guess, is 'When the going gets tough, the tough get going.'"

"That's the popular cliché, of course. But what I believe intensity means is that the 'tough' are already going strong, so when the going gets tough, they have enough momentum behind them to mow over the obstacles in their path."

"Wow! I never looked at it that way," Bob confessed. "That's great!"

"I'm glad you see it. My belief is that circumstances don't create men and women, but rather, men and women create their circumstances. Last-minute managers allow things to happen to them, while on-time, on-target managers make things happen."

Bob was puzzled. "Okay, how do they really do that?"

"I believe there are four keys:

- They lead by example.
- They serve others.
- They ask for the things they need from others.
- They welcome and appreciate the contributions of others.

"Here's an example. I'm a football fan. And I've noticed that a really good NFL quarterback can do all of those things in the space of twenty or thirty seconds."

"I watch a lot of football myself," Bob said, "but I'm afraid you've lost me on that one."

"I've seen it countless times. A quarterback gets sacked for a huge loss. He's bruised. He's hurting. But he goes right back into the huddle and tells the other ten guys what he needs from them on the next down. He calls the play, hands the ball off to a running back, and then it may even be necessary for him to throw a block that turns the play into extra yards. When the whistle blows the play dead, he congratulates his fellow players on a job well done and then he calls another play."

I'm floored! It sounds as though the Chief Effectiveness Officer has an actual life, Bob thought. But aloud he admitted, "I could use some additional explanation."

"It seems to me that the winning quarterbacks out there see the victory as the ultimate goal, but they also see each play as a part of the victory. If the play moves the ball a few more yards downfield toward the immediate goal—a touchdown—that play contributes to the win. But if there's no gain, or there's a loss—or even worse, a penalty—"

"There's no contribution toward the goal." Bob concluded triumphantly.

"Right again," the CEO agreed. "On the next play, then, they have another opportunity to make things happen. They never, ever lose their intensity. And through their own intense play, they inspire the other members of the team to reach for their best, too."

"Now I get it!" Bob announced. "Last-minute managers get so focused on the immediate moment that they lose sight of the big picture. The small defeats sap their intensity and they simply fail to perform. The intense players are focused on the game plan. They keep coming back into the game, determined to move the team toward the ultimate goal. Toward the win."

"You've got it. And I noticed that you said 'players' and not just 'player.' You obviously recognize that no quarterback, no matter how talented he is, can win the game on his own. And no team, no matter how skilled or devoted it is, can win without a good quarterback."

"What you're saying must be that intensity has to be part of a shared vision."

The CEO was pleased by what she heard. "Exactly! I think you're ready to consider the next 'right.' And that's **'Do it for the right results.'**"

Bob's puzzled expression was once again the CEO's signal to continue.

"Would you like to believe that you made the world a better place by virtue of your being here, Bob?"

"Yes! Of course! And I realize that the day-to-day decisions that I make as I interact with other people will have an impact on my ability to achieve that end."

"That's a great way to look at it. But let's look at the opposite side. Bob, one of the worst dilemmas a company ever has to face is layoffs. After all, no manager who seeks to do the right thing for the right results wants to put loyal people out of work."

"That's a tough decision," Bob agreed.

"Here's the thing, though. If a company—or even a department—is losing money, and if the losses could eventually bring the company to financial ruin, would you lay off a few people to save the jobs of many more? Or would you hang on, hoping for a turnaround?"

Bob pondered the question for a moment, then finally concluded, "Like I said, it's a tough decision."

"Okay, let's make it even tougher. Let's suppose that we have reason to believe the company can ultimately survive if we don't make any personnel cuts. But let's say that we have a group of angry stockholders who get together at the shareholders' meeting and demand that we do something drastic."

"That's easy. Our employees' jobs are more important than our stockholders' concerns."

"Good thought," the CEO conceded. "But what if one of the stockholders is an elderly person—your mom or dad maybe—who is counting on that investment in that company's stock to see him or her through the remaining years of life. What then? How are layoffs, or no layoffs, going to impact the results?"

"I don't know," Bob admitted.

"I don't know either. Don't you see? It all ties together. To solve that problem, you have to connect all of the 'rights' into one on-time, on-target decision. A last-minute manager is immobilized by fear. Usually, it's the *fear of making a wrong decision.* So he or she is going to procrastinate—avoid making *any* decision—and everyone could suffer as a result. A few employees could be laid off too late, the stock recovery could happen too late, a devastating loss of confidence in the company could be the result, the company could fail, and, ultimately, your mom or dad could lose every dime invested in the stock. Procrastination is a killer."

"It really *is* all connected!"

"It sure is," the CEO said. "So your assignment for tomorrow is to figure out what you'd do in this situation. Determine your priorities, then run through the Bill of Rights. I'm sure you'll come up with a great plan."

With that, she stood up to escort him to the door.

"What about the third P?" Bob wondered aloud. "You haven't told me about it yet. Wouldn't that be something that could help me with my decision?"

"Might be. But not right now. Your assignment is to figure it all out. The third P will help you know what to do after you've come up with the answer."

This hardly seems fair, Bob the Muttering Manager mumbled to himself as he left the CEO's office. *It would certainly help if I knew the third P.*

EIGHT

Deep in Thought

On his drive home, Bob pondered all of the things he had discussed with the CEO that day. *How do the "rights" in the Bill of Rights fit together to help me solve the problem posed by the CEO?* he wondered. *In fact, how do they fit together to solve* any *problem?*

Less than a half mile down the road, Bob passed a large billboard that bore the date "9/11/2001" and the words "We will never forget." Normally any event that had taken place that long ago would have been a fading memory by now, but that horrific day flashed through Bob's mind as vividly as if it had happened yesterday.

"That's it," Bob suddenly exclaimed aloud, as he recalled the brave actions taken by Todd Beamer, Jeremy Glick, Tom Burnett, and others on United Airlines Flight 93. *What a perfect example of the Bill of Rights—doing the right thing, for the right reasons, with the right people, at the right time, in the right order, with tremendous resolve and intensity, for the right results!*

Bob reconstructed the events of that fatal flight in his mind. The passengers had done the right thing by crashing the airplane in order to save countless other lives. They had done it for the right reasons, they had formed the right partnership among the passengers, and they had done it at the right time—far from heavily populated areas and well before the intended target could be hit. They had done it all in the right order: They had developed their alliance, formulated a plan, and jumped into action. And they had done it for the right results, even though their tragic deaths would seem to belie that fact.

Had they procrastinated in making their decision or in taking action—had no one but "Last-Minute Bobs" been on board that flight—the outcome would likely have been different. The aircraft could have slammed into the White House or the nation's Capitol building—and devastated the United States government. On-time and on-target decisions prevailed, but what a price those brave passengers paid. What a selfless act of courage!

Bob reflected on other high-profile news events in recent times. He thought about the various men and women who had done the wrong thing with the wrong people for the wrong reasons.

I'm really beginning to see how having clear priorities and then filtering them though the Bill of Rights could help me become on-time and on-target, Bob thought. *But does that mean I'll be able to conquer my tendency to procrastinate—to be a last-minute manager? There, I did it! I admitted that I probably am a last-minute manager.*

"How did it go with the CEO today?"

Bob the Occasionally Perceptive Manager positively knew his wife was going to ask that exact question when he walked through the door.

"Great," he assured her. "But I have a tough assignment tonight. All I have to do is keep our company afloat while it's losing millions of dollars, guarantee that no employees are laid off, and make certain that my mom doesn't lose any money on the stock she owns in the company."

"Your mother owns stock in your company?" Bob's suddenly confused wife asked.

"No, she doesn't. And we're not actually losing millions of dollars. Problem is, I don't walk on water, either. But with what I'm learning, I just might be able to do that someday!"

Bob slipped into his study, took out a legal pad and wrote:

PROBLEMS

- Company is losing money.
- Stockholders are angry.

POSSIBLE SOLUTIONS

- Lay off some employees; cut costs.
- Increase sales/revenues by going after new markets with improved products and customer service.
- Merge with a competitor.

POSSIBLE OUTCOMES

- The cuts save the company.
- The company makes a spectacular turnaround by going after new markets and introducing new products.
- The merger saves the company.
- Despite all efforts, stock falls. Big sell-off follows. Customer confidence plummets.
- Company goes out of business. Everyone loses his or her job.

Bob the Suddenly More Aware Manager experienced an almost supernatural revelation. *There are only two problems, but three possible solutions and five possible outcomes. Those seem like good odds! I think I can tackle that!*

What Bob didn't realize immediately was that both of the problems were negative, but only some of the solutions and outcomes were negative. When he finally recognized the situation, he dug out his notes and did his best to employ the ideas they contained.

The note at the top of the stack read:

PRIORITY: Priorities change. Know what to do and know when to do it. "Triage" the tasks at hand.

This strategy solves the first problem procrastinators face: LATENESS.

PROPRIETY: The Bill of Rights.

- Do the right thing.
- Do it for the right reasons.
- Do it with the right people.
- Do it at the right time.
- Do it in the right order.
- Do it with intensity.
- Do it for the right results.

This strategy solves the second problem procrastinators face: POOR QUALITY WORK.

Bob thought about the priorities. *I believe this company still offers a valuable product and good service. It also provides good jobs to some great people. So my priority would be to help make the company financially stable so it can continue to provide products, service, and jobs.*

With these thoughts clearly embedded in his mind, Bob took a look at the topic of propriety.

"Do the right thing." *Hmmm. I think the right thing would be to keep as many of its people employed as it can, while balancing that "right" with the rights of its customers and shareholders.*

Then an oddly on-target idea crossed Last-Minute Bob's mind. *If I were the president or CFO of this company, and I had been spending a lot of my time reading trade magazines and pursuing other low-priority activities, I wouldn't have been tracking trends. If I had tracked trends, I might have seen the downturn coming and could have solved at least part of the problem through natural attrition—retirements and resignations. Procrastination could have contributed to my present situation. Interesting how priority and the Bill of Rights are so tightly linked together.*

Bob moved on. The next "right" was a little more difficult. **"Do it for the right reasons."** *Job security is certainly one of them, but more that that, securing the financial futures of the company's people and its investors is a great reason to do the right thing,* Bob thought.

Bob's eyes fell to the next item on the list. **"Do it with the right people."** *I'm sure all of us must have been the right people at one time or another, or we wouldn't have been hired in the first place. So what should the company do? Solve the cutbacks issue through natural attrition? Would that happen quickly enough on its own? Or should the company offer early retirement? These issues are about human beings and their lives. This really* is *tough!*

Bob made a few more notes and continued. **"Do it at the right time."** *It seems to me that a last-minute manager is going to delay any decision until it's too late. So whatever I decide in any situation, I have to follow through at the right time. Does that mean right away? Or do I occasionally hold out, hoping for a change in the situation?*

Maybe the answer lies in the next "do it," Bob thought. **"Do it in the right order."** *Maybe the right order is to focus on sales, cut executive salaries and perks as a clear example that the company is serious about this, count on some attrition to help, and, as a last resort, proceed with layoffs.*

Bob worked through the remaining points on the Bill of Rights—**"Do it with intensity"** and **"Do it for the right results"**—and entered his plan on his computer. He was confident that the CEO would find it to be a carefully drawn plan.

But what's the third P? he wondered the next morning as he drove to work—and to his next appointment with the CEO.

NINE

Whose Alphabet Is It, Anyway?

"Let's take a look," the CEO said as Bob handed his thoughtfully executed plan to her. He sat in silence for several tense moments while she pored over the document.

Hope I didn't make any typos, he thought.

The CEO finally broke the silence. "Pretty solid plan."

Bob the Instantly More Confident Manager beamed. "Glad you like it."

"There's just one thing I'd like to know, though."

Uh-oh, Bob thought. "What is that?" he asked aloud.

"If you were the head of our company, how would you propose to pull this off?"

"I'd work on it step-by-step."

"But what if it didn't work the way you thought it would right away?"

"I'd change the plan then, I guess. Revise it. Do something else."

"That's what most managers would do," the CEO conceded. "But there's another option. It's the third P in the Three P Strategy."

Good! Bob thought. *I'm eager to learn about the third P!*

Again the lights dimmed. Again the screen scrolled down from the ceiling. Again the music swelled and the video projector flashed an image onto the screen. Again the "word of the moment" danced before Bob's eyes and ultimately stabilized on the screen, chiseled onto a stone tablet.

"Commitment."

That was the word on the screen. No other words. Just that one.

Not "Promise" or "Passion" or "Purpose" or "Pride." Not "Prerogative" or "Premise" or "Prudence."

No, this word clearly began with the letter "C." Throughout the recorded history of the English language, the word "commitment" has always begun with a "C."

"How can the third P begin with a 'C'?" Bob asked.

The CEO had heard that question more than a few times previously. "It's a memory device," she responded. "I've tried to find a word that begins with the letter P to complete the Three 'P' concept, but the only word that works for me begins with a 'C.' It all goes back to my dad. If he had understood that health was a priority, if he had recognized that he had to do the right things for the right reasons with the right partners for the right results, the eventual outcome may have been entirely different. But he was never committed to doing anything about his health."

"You're saying that there's really no third word that could begin with 'P'?" Bob the Politely Incredulous Manager asked.

"I've gone through three dictionaries and I've never found one word that expresses exactly what this is all about. Besides, if I gave you three words that begin with the letter 'P,' would you remember them all?"

"You're right. Probably not. But if I think of the Three P's as Priority, Propriety, and Commitment, I'm sure I'll never forget them."

"I know it sounds a little hokey," the CEO admitted, "but commitment is such an integral part of the formula that it deserves special attention."

"I know a lot of committed people," Bob interjected, "but some of them are committed to things that aren't important."

"Outstanding observation," the CEO said. "I believe that the people whose lives are the most tragic are those who are committed to insignificant things or to the wrong things. The pages of *The Guinness Book of World Records* are filled with the accomplishments of committed people who own the world's largest ball of yarn or who have eaten the most metal.

"And the pages of history books and today's newspapers are filled with the stories of people who were committed to an unjust cause or senseless violence. There are committed drug dealers, committed terrorists, and committed racists."

"I imagine this is somehow connected to procrastination?" Bob posed.

"It sure is. Procrastinators often get bogged down as the result of their inability to distinguish between the important and the unimportant, as well as between a worthy cause and an unworthy one."

"The difference must be the Bill of Rights," Bob suggested.

"You're exactly right, Bob. But what many people don't understand is the difference between 'interest' and 'commitment.' An interested person—for example, someone interested in exercise and fitness—can come up with all sorts of excuses as to why today isn't the right day. A committed person doesn't know about excuses. Commitment means the job gets done, no matter what. Not knowing the difference between commitment and interest causes a lot of stress for last-minute managers and the people who are counting on them."

"I understand what you're saying. Interest doesn't necessarily result in action, but commitment invariably does!"

The CEO smiled, opened a drawer in her desk, pulled out an envelope, and handed it to Bob.

"This is almost your last assignment," said the CEO. "Before long, you'll be going it on your own, to put the Three P strategy into practice."

"Will I still be able to see you if I have problems?" Bob asked.

"Of course. Plan to put in some time on this assignment, then come see me at the same time tomorrow."

"I'm on it! I'll see you tomorrow!"

TEN

Another Night of Thought

"I know it's been a challenge," Bob's wife said supportively after he had explained that he had yet another assignment to complete. "We've both always believed that the best things in life are worth the work we put into them. I know that part of the reason we have such great kids is because you worked so hard to advance in your profession so that I could give up my real estate career to be a full-time mom."

"Do you ever wish that we'd had our children in our twenties instead of our thirties so that you could have resumed your career plans?" Bob the Deliberately Last-Minute Procreator asked.

"Not for one second!" Bob's wife replied. "I admit I've been envious of other women who have built great careers the entire time their children have grown up, but they've been envious of the special times—the extra times—I've been able to enjoy with our kids. Everything is a trade-off, I guess."

"I guess it is. My trade-off is that I have to miss the game on ESPN and study the contents of this mysterious envelope."

It was Bob the Occasional Gourmet Cook's turn to prepare dinner, so he made his famous Caesar salad. The eggs must have been a tad on the old side, because his usual concoction didn't whip up quite as creamy as it should have.

After dinner, Bob went to his study and opened the envelope. He read a short but powerful story.

> The graduates of a small town high school returned to their hometown for their ten-year reunion.
>
> One of the classmates asked the others to answer a simple question: "Who was the person who most influenced your life while you were in school?"
>
> She expected to receive a wide range of answers—the principal, a coach, a favorite teacher—but when the answers were turned in, there was one clear choice.
>
> The janitor.
>
> The reason?

Every day, after everyone had gone home, the janitor cleaned the rooms and washed the whiteboards. Then, this man who had only completed fourth grade wrote three simple misspelled words on the upper left corner of the whiteboard: "YA GOTTA WANNA."

This man had inspired many generations of students to "wanna." But his simple statement raises a couple of questions.

"What do ya gotta wanna do?"

And "Why do ya wanna do it?"

Bob pondered the story for a few minutes. Then he brushed his teeth and went to bed. He laid there, wide awake, and asked himself over and over, *What do I wanna do? And why do I wanna do it?*

The next day, Bob the Exhausted from Staying Up Half the Night Manager lumbered into the CEO's office a full two minutes early and plopped into the nearest chair.

"I'll tell her you're here," the CEO's assistant offered. "But only if you really *are* here."

Bob looked at her with a puzzled expression.

She smiled and said, "You must be at the 'Ya gotta wanna' point in The Process."

"How did you know?"

"This is the one that keeps 'em all up at night," she replied. "I've seen it four times in just the last two weeks."

I wonder how many people the CEO is putting through this torture?

The CEO welcomed Bob into her office for what he intuitively knew was the final stage of The Process.

"What do you think?" the CEO began.

"I gotta wanna, I guess," Bob responded lamely.

"You can't *guess* ya wanna. Ya truly *gotta* wanna. That's what the third P is all about. It's about commitment. One of the wise sayings I've dug up says, 'Whatever your hand finds to do, do it with all your might.'"

"That's a great thought. But what does the management in our company expect me to be committed to, exactly?"

The CEO considered her response carefully. "We don't expect. We simply hope. We hope that you will take hold of the Three P Strategy and apply it every day. Our next hope would be that you're committed to yourself and to your family. If a job comes between you, your family, and your dreams, you're committed to the wrong priorities."

"So you're telling me that my family and I should come first in my life?"

"That's exactly it."

"I've always thought that in business, it was company first, family second."

"In my life, God comes first, my family and friends second, and my career third. If something doesn't go as well at work as I want, I still have something left over. People who see their self-worth as only related to their work are devastated by negative feedback, even if it's constructive. Why? Because they think their work is who they are. That makes their work life really stressful. When they have higher priorities, work is important—but it's not everything. That puts things in perspective. And perspective relieves stress."

"I can see how your point of view makes sense. If 'career' is at the top of this list, life could be pretty shallow and unfulfilling."

"I believe you're exactly right, Bob. Speaking only for myself, the Third P means:

- Commitment to God
- Commitment to Family
- Commitment to Priorities
- Commitment to Propriety

- Commitment to Purpose
- Commitment to Ideals
- Commitment to Goals
- Commitment to Integrity
- Commitment to Truth
- Commitment to Follow-Through."

Bob thought about what the CEO had just said. "Our time together has really opened my eyes to so many things I never considered before. I can see how your list truly comes from your heart. I'm beginning to understand why all of this is important, even though I don't know much about spiritual things. I have gone to my house of worship from time to time, but I've never thought about putting God on my list of priorities. I also believe I can now make my own list that expresses my personal priorities, my understanding of the Bill of Rights, and my commitment to things that really matter."

"I believe you can, too. All on-time, on-target managers understand the components of the Three P Strategy and apply them in their lives. It's obvious that you are really beginning to connect with what it all means and how it can impact your results."

The CEO opened the file drawer in the credenza behind her desk and pulled out another nine-by-twelve envelope. She handed it to a bewildered Bob and said, "I hold in my hand the last assignment! I have a strong feeling that your probation will come to an end very quickly."

Bob desperately tried to conceal his enthusiasm, but that wasn't possible. "Really? Great! What time do you want me back here tomorrow?"

"How about 1:00 P.M.? I'm starting The Process with a new person in the morning."

"One P.M. it is!"

ELEVEN

Not More of This!

"My probation is coming to an end soon," a triumphant Bob announced to his wife the minute he walked through the door.

"Wonderful!" she exclaimed as she began to smother him with hugs and kisses. "When will you know?"

It occurred to Bob that he couldn't answer that question. "I'm not sure. I have my last assignment, so the CEO must think I'm ready to 'graduate.'"

Bob and his family enjoyed dinner and conversation together. At about 9:30 P.M., he said good night to the kids and headed for his study. He opened the envelope. *Pretty straightforward,* he thought to himself as he surveyed the cover page. It read:

Answering the following questions is optional. The CEO welcomes the opportunity to review and discuss your answers with you, but you

> ***are under no obligation to do so. You might want to save your responses and refer to them in the future.***

Strange, Bob thought. He studied the second page. It contained several questions, preceded by these words:

> ***Please take the time to answer these questions before you come to the CEO's office for your appointment tomorrow. Doing so will help you apply the Three P's in your life and career.***

Bob was mightily tempted to ignore this part of The Process—since he didn't have to turn in these pages anyway. *Oh, wait!* he thought. *If I don't do this, that means I don't have much commitment, and that would make me a last-minute manager.*

Bob searched for a pen that worked, finally found one, and began to answer each question thoughtfully.

1. Describe your priorities as you perceive them to be at this moment.

2. How committed are you to those priorities?

3. What do you personally believe to be the most important aspect of propriety?

    - Do the right thing?

- Do it for the right reasons?
- Do it with the right people?
- Do it at the right time?
- Do it in the right order?
- Do it with intensity?
- Do it for the right results?

4. Can you define your personal vision? What is your purpose/mission? What is your picture of the future?
5. What are your most important values?
6. How committed are you to those values?
7. What are your short-term goals?
8. How about your long-term goals?
9. When it comes to integrity:
    - Are you committed to the truth?
    - Are you true to yourself?
10. Are you willing to follow through on your commitments?
    - No matter what the ultimate cost?
    - No matter what the potential consequences?

When he had finished answering the last question, Bob reviewed his answers. *There's no way I'm going to turn in this questionnaire,* Bob thought. *I need to keep this handy, as my reminder of what I'm going to be all about!*

When he walked into the CEO's office, Bob's first impulse was to say, "Yo! Bob the On-Time, On-Target Manager reporting for duty!" But he successfully fought off that impulse.

"Did you complete the questionnaire?" the CEO asked.

"Sure did," was Bob's confident reply.

"And?"

"I'm going to keep this as a personal reminder, but I do want to discuss my answers with you," Bob the Committed to a New Way of Doing Things Manager responded.

They spent a few minutes going over Bob's questionnaire, and it was obvious that the CEO was impressed by Bob's answers. As their meeting came to a close, she congratulated him on his hard work and assured him he was doing well.

Big brothers can be wrong sometimes, the CEO thought to herself as Bob walked out the door.

TWELVE

On-Time, On-Target

Bob the On-Time, On-Target Manager walked back to his office with a spring in his step that had been missing for quite some time.

One of the first things he did that day was post a note that would stare him in the face every time he glanced in the direction of his computer monitor.

All the note said, very simply, was:

PRIORITY. Triage everything.

PROPRIETY. Remember the Bill of Rights.

COMMITMENT. "I gotta wanna."

Despite the encouraging daily reminder, old habits were hard to break. Bob struggled for the longest time to adjust his priorities—and his schedule . . . his way of doing things—so that he could meet his commitments both at work and at home.

What helped Bob the most was the development of a daily triage form. Here he was able to write down his major commitments for the day, his essential tasks, e-mails, phone calls, and "gotta wannas."

Bob also made some immediate progress in other areas. For starters, he pulled into the gas station long before he needed a refill. Even if it was only down by a third or a half, if he had extra time, he filled the tank. From the day he made that decision, he never worried about running out of fuel on his way to an important meeting. He used the small gaps in his schedule to prioritize all of the small activities so that the big blocks of time could be invested more productively.

He also learned how to delegate—something he had never completely figured out before. The company had long ago provided a cell phone to every manager, but there never seemed to be enough time to program all of his frequently called numbers. *Aha!* he thought. *I'll have Michelle input all the numbers during her free time between school and dance practice.* That task took his daughter just over thirty-five minutes and he paid her a much-appreciated ten bucks.

One of the most impactful lessons he learned about applying the Three P Strategy occurred when the representative of a company that wanted to be added to his list of vendors paid him a visit.

TRIAGE PLAN FOR ______________________ 20____

MAJOR COMMITMENTS FOR TODAY

- [ ] ____________
- [ ] ____________
- [ ] ____________

ESSENTIAL TASKS TO FULFILL COMMITMENTS

- [ ] ____________
- [ ] ____________
- [ ] ____________

OFFICE DUTIES FOR THE DAY

- [ ] ____________
- [ ] ____________
- [ ] ____________

E-MAILS/LETTERS TO WRITE

- [ ] ____________
- [ ] ____________
- [ ] ____________
- [ ] ____________
- [ ] ____________
- [ ] ____________

MY GOTTA WANNAS

- [ ] **Exercise**
- [ ] ____________
- [ ] ____________
- [ ] ____________
- [ ] ____________
- [ ] ____________

PHONE CALLS TO PLACE/RETURN

- [ ] ____________
- [ ] ____________
- [ ] ____________
- [ ] ____________
- [ ] ____________
- [ ] ____________
- [ ] ____________
- [ ] ____________
- [ ] ____________
- [ ] ____________
- [ ] ____________
- [ ] ____________

"I can not only beat my competitors' prices by two percent," the visitor boasted, "but I can also offer you an ongoing 'personal management fee' of five percent that will be deposited directly into your personal checking account without anyone ever knowing about it."

Bob listened to the visitor and a quick string of "rights" raced through his mind. *He's offering me a kickback. It's not the right thing to do, it's not for any of the right reasons, and this clown certainly isn't the right partner.*

So Bob showed his visitor the door.

As time went on, Bob's schedule seemed to be packed beyond capacity, and there were often important things that remained undone at the end of each day—despite his increased ability to "triage."

Thankfully, however, he had developed tremendous trust in the CEO. She had the rare ability to see issues from a clear, unobstructed vantage point, so he decided to talk to her about the problem.

The CEO listened carefully, then, without warning, she pushed the magic button on her desk. As the lights dimmed, the screen dropped from the ceiling, and the music began to play, Bob said, "Don't tell me there's another P!"

The CEO smiled but didn't reply. She simply waited for her projector to do its thing. As had happened three times previously, a single word blazed and burned itself in stone. This time the word had only two letters—and the first letter wasn't "P." It was "N."

The word was "**No**."

Bob was astonished. "No?" he asked.

"Yes," the CEO responded. "More correctly, 'Yes and No.' On-time, on-target managers know *when and how to say yes,* and *when and how to say no*. Last-minute managers often get hopelessly behind because they believe the only appropriate answer to any request is 'Yes.' This gets back to the difference between interest and commitment. When you say 'yes' to something you are interested in doing, other people don't know that your 'yes' really means 'maybe.' It's okay to be interested in many things, but commitment should be reserved for only high priority activities where 'yes' really means 'yes' no matter what. So commitment adds intensity to high priorities."

Bob was genuinely puzzled. "If I say no to someone's request, doesn't my response demonstrate that I don't have a servant heart?"

"Not at all. People often feel that having a servant heart means that you have to please everyone. That is a misconception. Having a servant heart means that you always have the greater good in mind. It means you care about yourself, the company, your coworkers, and our customers more than you care about saying yes to satisfy what are often the selfish needs of those who are not in alignment with that philosophy. Just as it's not possible for darkness and light to exist in the same place at the same time, it's also not possible for selfishness and selflessness to coexist. And a last-minute manager cannot possibly live in the same body as an on-time, on-target person. The exciting part of this is, you get to decide what you want to be . . . and will continue to become."

"That really makes sense," Bob observed. "And I can see now that the Three P's will help me determine when to say yes, and when to say no."

"Exactly! The reason I only display 'No' on my screen is because that's the part of 'Yes and No' that gives people the most trouble. You must be able to apply the principle of triage, the Bill of Rights, and the 'Ya gotta wanna' approach to every 'Yes' and every 'No.' Otherwise some of your 'yes' answers may end up being 'maybes' and you create stress for yourself and others."

"I really appreciate your time," Bob said as he stood to leave. "This has been extremely helpful."

"Bob, there's something you should know. When you were first put on probation, you were late for our first meeting, and you rushed into the second meeting—completely out of breath. I should have called off The Process right then and there. But I really wanted to give you a chance. I've read about the things you've done for our community in the newspaper. I sensed that I was sitting across the desk from a quality individual—albeit a last-minute manager. Truthfully, I believed that somewhere underneath all of the last-minute habits, there was the heart of a caring servant. So I called my big brother and asked him if you were really worth keeping on the payroll. He said, 'Yes, if you can figure out how to transform him from a last-minute manager into an on-time, on-target manager.' Then he candidly admitted that he didn't know how to do that. He didn't believe that a Chief Effectiveness Officer could help solve the problem either, but you've proved him wrong."

Bob was baffled by her words. "You have an older brother? He works here? And I know him?"

The CEO smiled. "I didn't say I had an older brother. I said I had a 'big brother.' My big brother and his wife helped me through some troubled times in my life—right after my father died—when I was only twelve years old. My mom brought me to Big Brothers Big Sisters, a wonderful organization that helps kids who are in need of role models. That's where I met Dave and Beth."

"Dave? Beth?" Bob asked. "I know a Dave and Beth, believe it or not."

At this point, the CEO was grinning broadly. "You do, do you?"

It was as if lightning had struck him. "You don't mean . . . ?"

"Dave Pederson, our president and Chief Executive Officer . . . ?" the CEO coaxed.

"Yes, that Dave."

"That's the one. My Big Brother. And Beth is my Big Sister. I'm proud to be able to say that!"

"Wow! I never would have guessed!"

"Bob, they changed my life. They enriched me in ways I could never have imagined or predicted. As a result, I determined that I wanted to do everything I could to enrich the lives of others. I decided that the best way I could accomplish that was by being a CEO—in a way, a caring sister."

"I've never thought of you as a sister, but you've certainly changed my life. I am grateful to you for that!"

The CEO was pleased by what she had heard. "Bob, I would say your last ten months have been a success by every measure. If I've contributed in any way, I will feel rewarded."

"You have—in more ways than you could ever know."

"I'm glad."

Bob stood up to leave, but the CEO stopped him.

"Do you have just one more minute to spare?"

"Sure do," was Bob's reply.

"I have some big news to share, Bob, and I want you to be the first to hear it. I'm going to have a baby, and my husband and I are both thrilled."

"That's wonderful!" Bob exclaimed.

The CEO continued, "I've decided that my baby is going to be my top priority . . . so I will be leaving Algalon. With the exception of taking on a few speaking engagements, I plan to be a full-time mom."

Bob felt a sudden lump grow in his throat. "I'm really going to miss you. I hate to admit it, but you've become kind of a security blanket to me."

"You'll do great without me, Bob. You've become a wonderful on-time and on-target manager, and you're likely to remain that way."

"When's your last day here?"

"Two weeks from tomorrow."

"Can I buy you lunch before you leave?"

"I'd be honored," the CEO replied.

They parted company and Bob left work that day with a renewed sense of confidence in his ability to master his world, partly because he knew he could finally say "no," and partly because he suddenly realized that there are people in this world who enrich and empower others through their unselfish ways. *What a wonderful legacy she'll be leaving behind,* Bob thought as he drove home that afternoon.

Five hours later, though, as he was about to drift off to sleep, a troubling thought surfaced, seemingly out of nowhere.

I know "I gotta wanna." But what is it I gotta wanna do?

THIRTEEN

The Perfect Solution

At precisely 2:32 A.M., Bob awakened from his sound sleep with a start.

"That's it!" he exclaimed aloud.

"Mmmmm?" his wife mumbled as her pleasant dream was interrupted. "What's it?" she asked groggily.

A few minutes later, they were seated at the kitchen table sipping hot tea. Their conversation was intense. So much to consider. So many positives and negatives to weigh. After all, this would be a major change. A complete redirection.

"Do you think they'll go for it?" Bob's wife wondered aloud.

"I don't know. It's worth a shot, though. That's for sure."

Finally, at 4:49 A.M. Bob's wife smiled and said, "Bob, if you really wanna, you gotta go for it!"

• • •

When Bob the Tired from Lack of Sleep Manager arrived at work that morning, he immediately placed a call to the Chief Effectiveness Officer.

"Bob here. Any chance we could meet for lunch today?" he asked tentatively.

The CEO checked her schedule. "I'll have to move one meeting, but I'm sure I can do that, so you're on."

The lunch discussion went better than Bob could ever have imagined, and when he returned to his office, he phoned the HR Director. "Could the CEO and I meet with you for a few minutes sometime this afternoon?" She agreed, and the three of them settled on Bob's office at 2:15 P.M. *Perfect! That'll give me just enough time to put my thoughts in order on my computer.*

When they got together, Bob wasted no time getting to the heart of the matter. He handed an envelope to the HR Director. She opened it, and to her surprise, she pulled out Bob's revised résumé. The CEO simply sat there with a knowing grin on her face.

"Are you sure this is what you want, Bob?" the HR Director asked.

"It sure is. I really 'wanna'!"

The HR Director turned to the CEO. "What do you think of this?"

"I can't think of anyone better for the position. I'm convinced he'd be perfect."

"That's good enough for me," the HR Director said with a smile.

She placed a quick call to Dave and explained Bob's idea. When she got off the phone, she smiled and said, "Bob, I'm pleased to accept your application to be our new Chief Effectiveness Officer!"

Epilogue

A Personal Note from the Authors

Bob the Brand-New Chief Effectiveness Officer was far from perfect in his new position. He made sure he told everyone in the company, "We're in this together. We'll learn together, we'll grow together, and we'll succeed at becoming on-time and on-target together." One of the first things he did was to distribute small cards to every employee. They read:

THE THREE P'S OF THE ON-TIME, ON-TARGET PERSON:
PRIORITY. Triage everything.
PROPRIETY. Remember the Bill of Rights.
COMMITMENT. "I gotta wanna."

"Carry this card with you—or post it on your computer—as a reminder of how important the Three P's are to our business and to our personal success," he suggested as he handed out the cards.

Bob maintained an open-door policy, and said that he'd meet in off-site private, confidential sessions if that's what it took to help someone become on-time and on-target. As time went on, people opened up to him more frequently, and he became the glue that held struggling departments together.

Recognizing the importance of the Three P's, Bob persuaded the company to make The Process the central framework in the orientation program for all new employees.

Bob continued his predecessor's practice of leaving voicemail messages that all employees could dial up at their own discretion. He called them "Rich Moments," and they became the talk of the company.

He remained in close contact with the former CEO, because anytime he needed his "batteries recharged," he knew he could count on her. In fact, they decided to coauthor articles and deliver presentations about the functions of the Chief Effectiveness Officer so that more companies could develop on-time, on-target leaders.

In a personal sense, Bob's implementation of the Three P's also got him in tune with his physical and spiritual well-being. He remembered what the CEO had told him about her father, so Bob was determined not to miss the important events in Jared's and Michelle's lives—from graduation ceremonies to the birth of his first grandchild! His visits to his health club became more frequent and regular, and he even felt a need to develop his spiritual side.

Bob, like other On-Time, On-Target Managers, now knew who he was, where he was going, and what would guide his journey. He anticipated the changes and challenges—and confronted them head-on.

On-Time, On-Target Managers embark on their extraordinary journeys for the right reasons, with the right people, at precisely the right time, and for the right results. They do the right things along the path, all in the right order, and they do everything with tremendous intensity.

On-Time, On-Target Managers are committed to the journey as well as to the end result. They are committed to the vision. To the truth. To integrity. To the best interests of others.

They are dreamers.

Yet they are realists.

They are hopeful.

Yet they recognize the present situation.

They are listeners.

But they speak up when necessary.

They are caring.

But not careless.

They have replaced selfishness with selflessness.

In essence, they have servant hearts.

Bob the Former Last-Minute Manager ultimately discovered that he needed to respond to the needs and longings of his family—and serve his wife and children.

Sometimes there's pain associated with the decision to live by the Three P's. The On-Time, On-Target Manager does not always experience smooth sailing. There were times when Bob's best efforts seemed to have little if any impact. There were other times when he got off track himself. But he was guided by "Ya gotta wanna," and that kept him from becoming discouraged.

The most important thing you should know is simply this: No matter how good your intentions, if you procrastinate as a regular habit—if you fail to triage your responsibilities, if you ignore the Bill of Rights, and if you lack in commitment—you could be flirting with disaster.

We believe that if you study the personal and corporate "Crash and Burns" of this world, you'll discover that procrastinators move to the head of that class in terms of flawed behaviors that lead to failure. Why? Because they fail to understand the essential nature of the Three P's.

If this story has paralleled your life in any way, we want to be the people who give you hope! You can conquer the affliction of procrastination. You can become on-time and on-target in every area of your life!

But Ya Gotta Wanna . . .

. . . Because No One Else Can Wanna for Ya.

—*Ken and Steve*

You Can Make a Difference. . . .

A young person's Big Brother or Big Sister can become his or her "Chief Effectiveness Officer" and make a positive impact that lasts a lifetime. This is something you can do! For information on how you can become involved in Big Brothers Big Sisters, go to their web site, www.bigbrothersbigsisters.org, or call toll-free at 1-888-412-BIGS.

Acknowledgments

At the risk of accidentally overlooking someone who deserves recognition, we would like to acknowledge and praise the following people for their involvement in our lives and in this book:

To Henry Ferris, our dedicated and talented editor, who "got" the important message of this book right from the beginning; his assistant, Lisa Nager, who was a delight to work with; and Michael Morrison, publisher of William Morrow, who has become a real supporter of this project.

To Richard Andrews and Humberto Medina, for their savvy business minds, which helped us immeasurably in developing win-win contracts.

To Sheldon Bowles, one of the most supportive and creative people in the world, who encouraged Steve from the beginning.

To Alan V. Brunacini, chief of the Phoenix Fire Department and author of *Essentials of Fire Department Customer Service*, for sharing with us his mission, his vision, and his values.

To Dottie Hamilt and Anna Espino, Ken's talented support team, for always being there for us.

To Martha Lawrence, writer and editor extraordinaire, for her constant support and help in the final stages of this project.

To Norman Vincent Peale for his insights about The Ethics Check.

To Dr. Robert Stadheim for teaching us that no one else can "wanna for ya."

To Jesse Stoner for what she taught us about vision.

To Art Turock for what he taught us about the difference between commitment and interest.

And Steve has some special praisings he wants to give.

Thanks to the following supportive friends who have earned my gratitude in so many ways:

Father Duane Pederson, Rosey Grier, Estean Hanson Lenyoun III, Dave Gjerness, Michael Clifford, Senator Dave Durenberger, Pam and Gary Benoit, Scott Blanchard, Kathy Styer, Ken and Susan Wales, Doug and Sandy Ross, Samuel Lopez de Victoria, John Hanson, Don Stolz, and Terry Esau.

Thanks to Dave Johnson and Theresa Lynch, my flight instructors, for teaching me the meaning of "ya gotta wanna."

I am also grateful to Richard Baltzell, a long-time friend in the publishing field, who patiently answers my questions and guides me through a variety of processes.

I cannot overlook Walt Kallestad, Paul Sorensen, and Tim Wright for reasons that they all know well.

And special thanks to Ole Loing, my "encourager" and seventh grade English teacher who convinced me that I really could construct a coherent sentence and didn't have to settle for a "D" in his class.

Both of us want to recognize our wives, Margie and Karla, for their inspiration and encouragement, and our children, Scott and Debbie Blanchard (and Debbie's husband, Humberto), Jonathan and Michelle Gottry (and her husband Jared), and Kalla Paige for their love and support.

We both believe that it's really God who's the author of the Three P Strategy—to Him we are eternally grateful.

About the Authors

KEN BLANCHARD is the chief spiritual officer of The Ken Blanchard Companies, a worldwide training and development firm. He is the author of several best-selling books—including the blockbuster international bestseller *The One Minute Manager*® and the giant business best-sellers *Whale Done!, Raving Fans,* and *Gung Ho!*—which have combined sales of more than thirteen million copies in more than twenty-five languages. He also codeveloped Situational Leadership® II—among the world's most practical, effective, and widely used leadership programs on the market today. Few people have made a more positive and lasting impact on the day-to-day management of people and companies as Ken Blanchard. He and his wife, Margie, live in San Diego and work with their son Scott, daughter Debbie, and her husband, Humberto Medina.

Services Available

The Ken Blanchard Companies is a global leader in workplace learning, employee productivity, and leadership effectiveness. Building upon the principles of Ken's books, the company is recognized as a thought leader in leveraging leadership skills and recognizing the value of people in accomplishing strategic objectives. Through seminars and in-depth consulting in the areas of teamwork, customer service, leadership, performance management and organizational change, The Ken Blanchard Companies not only helps people learn but also ensures that they cross the bridge from learning to doing.

If this story inspired you to learn more about the Three P Strategy, go to www.kenblanchard.com/ontime-ontarget to download a free audio message from Ken and Steve. To learn more about the high impact training programs that reinforce the book's core management philosophies and practices, visit the web site or contact the company directly at:

The Ken Blanchard Companies
125 State Place
Escondido, CA 92029
Phone: 800.728.6000 or 760.489.5005
Fax: 760.489.8407
Web site: www.kenblanchard.com

STEVE GOTTRY was the founder and president of Gottry Communications Group, Inc., a full-service advertising agency and video production firm based in Minneapolis, Minnesota. He formed the company in 1970 and served a variety of organizations across the nation. Among his clients were HarperSanFrancisco, Career Press, Zondervan Publishing House, Prudential Commercial Real Estate, Warner Bros., World Wide Pictures, United Properties, Alpha Video, NewTek, Inc., Pemtom Homes, and Standard Publishing. His firm was the winner of a number of national awards, including three Silver Microphones for radio and awards for direct mail and film from the International Advertising Festival of New York.

In May of 1991, his agency was named "Small Company of the Year" by the Bloomington Chamber of Commerce. Steve was recognized as the "Small Business Advocate of the Year" by the Chamber in 1995.

Steve is the coauthor (with Linda Jensvold Bauer) of *A Kick in the Career*, and the author of *Common Sense Business in a Nonsense Economy*, originally published by Pfeiffer & Company, San Diego, in 1994. He has coauthored a novel, and has also written a book to help would-be screenwriters develop stories. He has written the screenplays for four produced television and video/DVD projects, and also writes, produces, and directs commercial and industrial video projects.

He and his wife, Karla, moved their family to Arizona in 1996 to leave the colder climate of Minnesota for 320 days of warm sunshine per year (on average)! He teamed up with Ken Blanchard in October 1998 to collaborate on a number of publishing projects.

Steve is a member of Dobson Ranch Toastmasters (Mesa, Arizona), an instrument-rated pilot, an avid semipro photographer, and a devoted Arizona Diamondbacks fan. He loves the outdoors and prefers to write in beautiful Sedona, at a remote campsite, near the ocean, or simply "out by the pool."

For more information, please contact:

Steve Gottry
Priority Multimedia Group, Inc.
P.O. Box 41540
Mesa, AZ 85274–1540
Phone: 480.831.5557
Fax: 480.831.7373
E-mail: steve.gottry@ontime-ontarget.com
Web site: www.ontime-ontarget.com

Find Out More

In 1979 Ken Blanchard founded The Ken Blanchard Companies to support organisations looking to put the principles of his books into practice. Now a major international management consultancy and training organisation, the company works with many of the world's leading businesses to unleash the full power and potential of their people. The Ken Blanchard Companies is perhaps best known as the originator of the most widely used leadership development process, Situational Leadership® II and also specialises in Team Building, Organisational Change and Customer Service. Consultancy services, in-house training, public workshops, coaching, speakers and a wide variety of learning materials are also provided through a network of offices in 30 countries worldwide.

You can contact The Ken Blanchard Companies directly at:

The Ken Blanchard Companies
Blanchard House
1 Graham Road
Wimbledon
London SW19 3SW

Tel: 020 8540 5404
Fax: 020 8540 5464
Email: uk@kenblanchard.com
Website: www.kenblanchard.com